Haunted Places
of
Wiltshire

Rupert Matthews

COUNTRYSIDE BOOKS
NEWBURY BERKSHIRE

First published 2004
© Rupert Matthews 2004

COUNTRYSIDE BOOKS
3 Catherine Road
Newbury, Berkshire

To view our complete range of books,
please visit us at
www.countrysidebooks.co.uk

ISBN 1 85306 879 9

Cover picture from an original
painting by Anthony Wallis

Designed by Peter Davies, Nautilus Design

Produced through MRM Associates Ltd., Reading
Printed by J. W. Arrowsmith Ltd., Bristol

• Contents •

HAUNTED PLACES OF WILTSHIRE

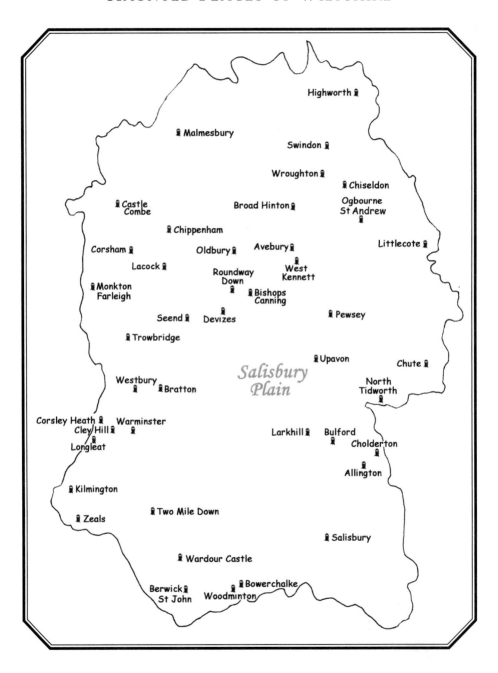

· Introduction ·

Wiltshire is possibly the most historic county in England. For over 5,000 years, almost every generation has left its mark here. There are circles of standing stones – including the most famous of them all at Stonehenge – and earthwork fortifications erected during long-forgotten wars. There are Roman ruins, Saxon buildings and castles, and grand houses and mansions from every age down to our own.

And, of course, there are the ghosts.

No county can claim a range of phantoms as broad as that which stalks Wiltshire. The county includes some of the oldest ghosts in England. The tall man who haunts the ancient burial mound of West Kennett may be older than Stonehenge itself. He and his hound have welcomed the rising sun over the high downland for millennia. Far more modern is the smartly suited gentleman sometimes glimpsed among the crowds of shoppers in central Salisbury. If he did not vanish with alarming suddenness into thin air, he might be mistaken for just another businessman.

There are some people, of course, who don't believe ghosts exist.

One such was a swimmer at the Westbury Public Baths. She tells me that, if she had thought about ghosts at all, it was as amusing but nonsensical characters in children's TV shows and books. And then she met George, the resident phantom of the baths. Now she knows that ghosts do exist but, as she told me, 'I've no idea what they are, just that I saw one.'

It would be too much to hope that all sceptics actually see a phantom and so become convinced of the reality of those that walk in Wiltshire. There are too many sceptics and too few spooks for that. But if any county will persuade doubters that there are such things, it is Wiltshire. So, take this book in your hands and set out to investigate for yourself.

Rupert Matthews

LONGLEAT

O f all the great houses of Wiltshire, few are as famous, as grand, or as haunted as Longleat House. The house is also remarkable as it has been home to the same family since it was built in 1568.

The estate, named after the stream of Long Leat, was a friary during the Middle Ages, but after the dissolution of the monasteries by King Henry VIII, the land was bought by Sir John Thynne, a land owner and dealer of genius. Sir John paid just £53 for the estate and then proceeded to spend £8,016 – a colossal sum – on the house.

The house, which was completed in 1580, has stayed remarkably unchanged ever since, though the state room rooms were updated in 1807. Longleat remains the earliest and most complete example of a Renaissance house in England. The architect, Robert Smythson, abandoned most features of the traditional English medieval manor, though he kept a great hall. He built instead a symmetrical house on a rectangular pattern, with large glass windows set into plain stone façades.

By the mid-18th century, the Thynnes' wealth and social standing had increased to such an extent that they had acquired the title of Viscount Weymouth. Thomas Thynne, the 2nd Viscount, married Lady Louisa Careret. As part of the wedding arrangement, Lady Louisa was allowed to bring her own servants to Longleat. One servant was a young footman whose devotion to his lady soon set tongues wagging.

Lady Louisa's husband, Thomas, suspected she was having an affair with the young footman and confronted the man in the passageway outside the old library. The viscount lost his temper and flung the footman down the spiral

Longleat House, the beautiful home of the Marquis of Bath, where one of the family ancestors returns in spectral form.

staircase that descends from that corridor. The servant's neck broke as he landed. It is said that Viscount Weymouth hurriedly had the man buried, telling his wife that the footman had left to attend to some family business of his own.

Lady Louisa, however, did not believe the story and became convinced that her husband had locked the faithful servant up in one of Longleat's many rooms. Evening after evening, Lady Louisa would prowl the corridors knocking on doors, forcing open locked doors, and tapping on panelling trying to find a hidden chamber. In the course of one such nocturnal ramble, Lady Louisa caught a chill that developed into pneumonia and caused her death.

Soon afterwards, her phantom was seen touring the corridors, knocking on doors. Today, known as the Grey Lady, the poor distraught ghost of Lady Louisa is the spectre seen most often at Longleat.

In 1903, when central heating was being installed at the house, it was necessary to lower the floor in the cellars to allow room for the boiler and piping. Just beneath the flagstones, a skeleton was found. The bones were gathered up and buried in the local church. Only later was it realised that the unknown body – presumably that of the footman – had been buried only a few feet from the 2nd Viscount Weymouth.

A second ghost lurks in the red library. Appropriately enough, this phantom sits quietly reading and bothers nobody. A third spectre is reported to run along corridors at night banging on the doors as if in great distress. No stories are attached to these phantoms. As with so many ghosts, they just appear, go about their business, and then vanish again, leaving the hapless witness none the wiser.

The gardens at Longleat have undergone numerous changes since they were laid out in a formal Italianate pattern by Smythson. In the 18th century Lancelot 'Capability' Brown remodelled the grounds as an arcadian park, and during the past 30 years the grounds have again been transformed, this time into a vast leisure attraction for the paying public. There is a safari park, the world's longest hedge maze, and an imitation medieval castle.

Through all the changes that have been made to the grounds, however, one feature has remained constant. The Green Lady continues to walk the grounds of Longleat no matter what planting scheme surrounds her. Opinions vary as to who this person might be, for nobody is really certain.

CLEY HILL

The looming bulk of Cley Hill dominates a large area of Wiltshire. Its summit is topped by ancient earthworks which are now in the care of the National Trust. As befits such a prominent landmark and ancient site, Cley Hill has attracted a fair share of legends.

It is said that many years ago the Devil himself came to Wiltshire. Striding across the landscape from Somerset, the Devil was heading for Devizes. The people there had turned their back on the evil one and embraced Christianity, and now the Devil was out for revenge. He carried over his shoulder a huge sack of earth with every intention of dumping this on the town that had so angered him.

As he walked, the Devil met an old man coming the other way. The Devil asked the man how far it was to Devizes. Suspecting the Devil was up to no good, the elderly farmer replied, 'Why, it is a great distance. I left there when I was a young man and look at me now.' The Devil looked. Deciding he did not dislike Devizes enough to travel for years to get there, he dumped the soil where he stood. And so Cley Hill was formed.

The link with the Devil may indicate that this hill was a stronghold of the old pagan religion. The obvious conflict with Christianity in the tale makes this supposition more likely.

Lying on the side of the hill is a great sarsen stone, the same sort of stone used to build Stonehenge and Avebury. Local legend has it that the face of the Devil is carved on the underside of the stone and that great misfortune awaits whoever turns the stone and reveals the evil one. Perhaps sensibly, nobody has turned the stone.

A further legend is less laden with doom. This concerns the ancient burial mound which stands on top of the hill. This barrow is said to be the home of the guardian spirit of local livestock. It is this spirit which presides over nearby Hog's Well, water from which is said to be a sure cure for sick pigs and will also ease sore eyes in humans. The spirit itself has been seen on occasion. He takes the form of a dwarf who lurks on the summit of Cley Hill around dusk. If you encounter such a phantom, it is probably best to examine it for horns and cloven hooves before speaking to it. Cley Hill is not the sort of place on which to make a mistake.

The legend-ridden Cley Hill, where danger lurks for the unwary.

CORSLEY HEATH

There are three ghosts at Corsley Heath. Rather sensibly they all gather at the welcoming Royal Oak inn, which stands beside the main road on the edge of the village.

The Royal Oak at Corsley Heath has some very active ghosts.

The oldest of the phantoms comes from the Middle Ages, when this building was a hospice which provided food and lodging to passing pilgrims and other travellers. It was owned and operated by the holy men of Long Leat Friary, on whose lands the beautiful Longleat House was later built.

One of the friars tasked with running the hospice that is now the Royal Oak was less than holy and distinctly dishonest. Rather than caring for the pilgrims who passed this way, he was inclined to ply them with ale and then rifle their pockets for money while they slept. He was also said to have pilfered the funds provided by the friary for the running of his establishment.

Disgraceful as such crimes might be, particularly in a man of holy orders, the punishment meted out to the friar of Corsley Heath does seem a bit severe. He was walled up alive in the cellar and left to die. His body remains there still, and his ghost returns from time to time. Perhaps he seeks forgiveness for his sins. There is a spot on the wall where a face can appear and then fade away. It may be shadows playing on the rough surface of the wall, but the bar staff are adamant. 'We tried painting over the area to get rid of it,' reported one, 'but then it came back. It isn't shadows or stuff. It is a face on the wall.'

The sad phantom of the friar in his long robes is seen upstairs in the bar as well. He stands quietly in the main bar, the oldest part of the building. The morose figure stares out of the window at the passing traffic for a while and then fades from sight.

Seen more often than the old monk is a lady who strides confidently about the pub. Wearing a dark dress that reaches to her ankles, this lady has a wide-brimmed hat on her head. She is without doubt a lady, rather than a maid or servant. Those who see her are aware of an unmistakable aura of elegance and culture that the ghost somehow emits.

A typical sighting occurred in the late summer of 2003. 'Our barman was going upstairs to fetch something,' reports the landlady. 'He was halfway up the stairs when the lady appeared on the landing and started down. He stepped aside to let her pass, just as you would if it were a real person. He told me he knew it was the ghost, but somehow did not quite realise it – if you see what I mean. It was like she was entirely natural. It was not until the lady had passed him and walked through the door at the foot of the stairs that he realised what had happened. Of course, he wasn't frightened a bit. Our lady is not scary at all. She is a proper lady.'

Quite who the ghostly lady might be is unclear. The locals are agreed that she has something to do with the days when the Royal Oak was a coaching inn on the Warminster road. Certainly her costume dates her to the early 19th century, before railways deprived country inns of the passing trade brought by long-distance stagecoaches. Some say she is the landlady of those days, others that she was a regular visitor on the coaches who now returns to her favourite inn. Whoever she is, she has been around for some time. 'We've been here some years and the landlord before us was as well,' confirmed the landlady. 'So that takes us back about 25 years. Our lady has been active all that time, and before as well, no doubt.'

The third ghost at the Royal Oak is more enigmatic. This is a white thing in the kitchen. It does not seem to take on any particular shape and is quite insubstantial. It does, however, get the blame for the fact that the kitchen lights are switched on and off without human action but with annoying regularity. 'The last time was about 6.30 one evening,' the barmaid said. 'It was broad daylight, but that light just came on of its own accord anyway.'

WARMINSTER

For such an ancient town, Warminster is surprisingly free of the supernatural, but it does have its moments. The town was founded long before the Norman Conquest and may date back to Roman times, though archaeology has yet to turn up any real Roman finds. The town was a royal manor in Saxon times, but it really came into its own with the wool trade in the 14th century. It was then that the local monastery was prosperous enough to build the magnificent minster church that still dominates the town, though it was much altered in the 19th-century restoration.

From this period also dates the ghost of Warminster. What is now St John's Street was then the centre of the monastic complex of buildings. It is, therefore, no wonder that it is here that the phantom monk walks. He does not seem to have any particular purpose for his haunting, nor a preferred spot in which to appear or vanish. Suddenly there he is. Then, just as inexplicably, he is gone.

The site of a second haunting would appear now to have vanished. Back in the days of the Merry Monarch, Charles II, a farmer from Salisbury Plain came to Warminster to sell the wool sheared from his sheep up on the windy grasslands. The farmer, William Lawne, did well and filled his purse with gold and silver coins. He stopped in Warminster for ale and food before setting off to walk home. Unfortunately for him, the ostler at the inn where he dined saw

The Warminster Monk has been seen walking around the site of the long-vanished monastery.

just how much gold he had on him and decided to get it for himself. As farmer Lawne travelled home, he was overtaken by the ostler and set upon. Lawne put up a fight and was killed for his troubles. The murderous horseman was subsequently caught and hanged from a gibbet on the site of the attack.

It is said that the gibbet remained for many years and was used for subsequent hangings. It stood on what is now the B3414, the road up to Salisbury Plain through Boreham. Long after the gibbet was taken down, when public hangings were abolished, the spot where it had stood remained bare earth, for nothing would grow there. And the phantom of farmer Lawne was said to lurk around the place.

These days, the road and its verges are covered in tarmac and concrete, and so it is impossible to locate the barren spot. If the phantom of the murdered farmer could help by pointing some phantom fingers, he has chosen not to, for he has not been seen in recent years.

WESTBURY

The little market town of Westbury is a quiet and charming spot. The Georgian houses which dominate its centre speak of a past prosperity, but, though this was real enough, it had little to do with the market or the surrounding rich acres. Westbury was the centre of glove-making in southern England for several generations in the 17th and 18th centuries.

The glove trade has passed away as a result of mechanisation and changing fashion, but one reminder of those days dominates not just the town but the whole valley. Carved on a hillside about a mile away is a white horse. It is in a highly visible position and when the sun dips down to the western horizon the horse can glow with an eerie red light as if bathed in blood.

If local legend is to be believed, this horse is not merely a chalk figure but a phantom horse of terrifying appearance, which goes by the name of the Moon Stallion. This powerful horse, locals believe, leaves its hillside on moonlit evenings to take on three-dimensional form as a gigantic spectral stallion. It then gallops off over the downs, past the enigmatic stone circle at Avebury, and along the ancient Ridgeway road, which was old when the Romans came here. Eventually, the Moon Stallion reaches the white horse of Uffington. The two horses stay together for the night, before the Moon Stallion retraces its path to Westbury and takes up its place above the town.

The Westbury White Horse, perhaps one of the oldest in England.

There is nothing to be seen in the white horse to indicate either that it is a stallion or that it has anything to do with the moon. It is a graceful and elegant horse, almost certainly a thoroughbred. But the white horse of Westbury was not always as it appears today. The current horse was cut in 1778 by servants of Lord Abingdon and was paid for by local worthies from their glove money. The old horse was a very different creature. It had a long neck and perky, upright ears. The body was long and low-slung, rather like that of a dachshund, and carried unmistakable signs that this was a male horse. The tail was lifted in an arch as if swishing flies aside and ended in a crescent, not unlike a moon.

How ancient the old horse truly was is unknown, but it is likely it had been there for many generations when it was destroyed in the recutting. The sweeping curves of its design are reminiscent of the design of the Uffington white horse. The two horses are also alike in that the hills on the slopes out of which they are carved are crowned by Celtic hillforts dating to pre-Roman days. Although it is now impossible to study the old Westbury horse, the Uffington figure can be investigated. Modern dating techniques indicate that it is around 2,500 years old. The similarities would indicate that the Westbury horse, too, is ancient.

It may be that the old stories suggest a religious link between the two Celtic hill horses. The truth is impossible to know, unless one evening you are up on the Wiltshire Downs and encounter the dramatic Moon Stallion galloping towards Uffington.

The human spectre of Westbury is decidedly homely by comparison with the dramatic Moon Stallion, and much more recent. Built in 1887, the Westbury Public Baths were a gift to the town from the wealthy mill owner William Laverton, who wished to give his native town a bequest of real practical worth. These are the oldest public baths in Britain still in use, though only the swimming pool remains in daily use. The bathtubs in which local families too poor to have their own could wash themselves have long since been removed.

For many years now the baths have been haunted by a man who goes by the name of George. This is not his real name, for nobody really knows who he is. George appears dressed in stained and soiled overalls and a collarless shirt.

The public baths at Westbury are the oldest in England, and also the most haunted.

Clearly he is a workman from the years before the Second World War, and some claim he is the phantom of the man employed to stoke the boilers that heated the waters here. This dutiful man apparently died young. Others dispute this account, saying that records from the time do not show the ghost walking soon after the man's death. In truth, the identity of the ghost of the Westbury Public Baths is unknown. Whoever he is, he is no bother to anyone. He potters about the corridors and side rooms on business of his own.

BRATTON

The village of Bratton is a deceptive place. It lies astride the B3098, just east of Westbury, where the road dips down suddenly to skirt the lower slopes of the plateau known as Salisbury Plain. To the casual driver passing on his way across the Wiltshire countryside, it appears as quiet and peaceful a village as any in the county. Yet this is a place steeped in history and in ghostly goings on. There is more here reaching out from the past than you will find in many towns.

The first phantom to be met near the village is one that appears in several places across Wiltshire and, indeed, England. Although it goes by various names, the Black Dog always fits a set description and it is universally held to be a most dangerous phantom to meet. This particular Black Dog lurks near St Catherine's Well. As elsewhere, it is said to be not just big, but enormous

– almost as big as a donkey. Its eyes are perfectly circular, more like saucers than eyes, and may glow with a dull red flame. This is a beast best avoided. If it is encountered, it is wise to get out of its way, for the Black Dog, or Shuck as it is often called, can cause sickness and death with terrifying ease.

Another harbinger of death lurks at Bratton. Where the main road through the village drops down to the bottom of the slopes of Salisbury Plain, it crosses a small stream. On nights of the full moon, a phantom hearse passes across this stream if a villager is to die before the next full moon. The best time to see the ghostly carriage is, apparently, at midnight. Not so long ago a group of local teenagers sat up on the night of the full moon. They saw nothing. But then none of the village's inhabitants died that month.

Rather higher up the hill is a short stretch of road said to be haunted by a pedlar from the 18th century. These men toured the villages carrying a stock of ribbons, buttons, and other frivolities that local women would buy from them

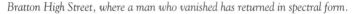

Bratton High Street, where a man who vanished has returned in spectral form.

Bratton's Stradbrooke Lane, where Flowers Farm used to stand.

rather than make a special trip into Devizes. This particular pedlar had done well on his week-long tour of the villages, but he never returned to his house in Bratton. It is widely presumed that he was murdered for his money and that his body was hidden too well to be discovered. Whether his ghost tries to lead the way to his remains or marks the spot of his murder is unknown, as nobody has yet been brave enough to follow him to find out.

In Stradbrooke Lane, there used to be a building named Flowers Farm. This Victorian house was demolished a few years ago, apparently because of its evil reputation. Doors slammed shut or opened of their own accord; footsteps echoed in empty rooms and over all was a feeling experienced by several visitors that something was not quite right about the house. In the course of the demolition, it was found that about 3 feet of the end of one bedroom had been blocked off. There was nothing in the space to explain the ghosts or the feeling of unease. Whatever it was has now gone and no strange occurrences have been reported since the house was pulled down.

A final historic link is found not in the village but the hills to the south. It was here in AD 878 that one of the most dramatic battles in English history was fought. On these heights King Alfred the Great finally and convincingly defeated the great army of the Vikings, thus saving England both for the English and for Christianity. There are no reported phantom Vikings from this battle, but a skirmish earlier in the campaign has left its ghostly mark on Wiltshire, as described on page 64.

TROWBRIDGE

T rowbridge is a busy town, which built its prosperity on a weaving industry that began in the 14th century and reached its peak of production in the 18th century. During the 19th century increasing mechanization in the mills of Lancashire and Yorkshire took away much of the trade. Today, the town is a thriving centre for surrounding villages, with a one-way system the signing of which seems designed to confuse strangers.

Trowbridge's Church Street is haunted by an evil ghost.

19

Church Street is now part of the one-way system and has a car park opening onto it. These combine to ensure that it is thronged with motorized traffic, often passing at high speed, while passers-by on foot are rather rare. This might be just as well, for pedestrians are apt to be bothered by a disturbing phantom known as the Old Hag of Church Street. This unpleasant ghost is one of the few phantoms that it really is best to avoid, and, if met, she should be left behind as quickly as feet can move. She is described as being old, very old, with wizened features and grotesquely wrinkled skin, and lacking most of her teeth. She wears a tatty coat or cloak of some dark material. It is the eyes, however, which attract most attention. They are bright and glitter whatever the weather.

This old woman exudes a feeling of naked and unrestrained evil. She is a nasty woman, who manages to drip hostility and malevolence simply by being there. Who she was in life and why her phantom is so unpleasant, nobody seems to know. And it is certain that no one is going to hang about to ask her.

Less unpleasant but rather more troublesome, in a practical sense, was the poltergeist of Roundstone Street. The poltergeist was active in a shop during the 1990s, when it indulged in typical poltergeist activity by knocking on doors, hiding objects, and moving the shop's stock around in a most annoying way. It was reported that the manifestations were linked to the fact that the upper rooms of the house had once been the nursery for the family that built the shop in late Victorian times. Perhaps it was a mischievous child who was responsible for the disturbances.

MONKTON FARLEIGH

The King's Arms in Monkton Farleigh claims to be the most haunted pub in Wiltshire, and with good reason. If the rumours are true, there are more ghosts here than it is possible to count.

Maria, the barmaid on duty one autumn evening in 2003, knew all about the most active of the ghosts. Well she might, having lived in the village all her life. 'We've all heard him,' she said, 'but not seen him, no. Well, nobody ever does. It happens when we are here in the bar getting ready to open up or clearing up after people have gone. I suppose he might be about at other times, but it's too noisy with all the customers in to hear him. Anyway, it starts with a sound like a door shutting. Then we hear great heavy footsteps walking along the corridor up there,' she pointed at the ceiling of the bar. 'He walks along in what sounds like heavy old boots. Stomp, stomp, stomp. Till he gets to the front. Then he stops. There is nothing there – no room or anything – just the window out front. It's all quiet for a bit. Then you hear the sound like of a woman crying, like she is really upset about something. But you can't tell where the noise is coming from. Might be upstairs, might not. It's right weird.'

Weird, indeed. But then the King's Arms is no stranger to odd events. Back in 1991, the downstairs of the pub was undergoing some building work to convert what had been odd rooms and outhouses at the rear into a comfortable dining area. The plan was to serve the customers with quality and hearty meals in comfortable surroundings, in place of the snacks served previously in the bar. The plan worked for the Chancel Restaurant which is still one of the favoured dining places of the area. In the course of the work an internal wall was due to be knocked down. Just days before the work began, a pair of strangers, unfamiliar to the staff, arrived. Without ordering anything, they informed the bemused and rather startled barmaid: 'No good will come of this work. Better not do it.' Then they left.

The fireplace in the King's Arms features in one of the eerie tales centred on this welcoming pub.

The work went ahead, and two discoveries were made almost at once. The first was that behind the wall was a second wall, in which was built an old fireplace. This was preserved and is now in regular and warming use during the winter months. The second was that bricked up within the wall was a small wooden box, in which was an ancient key. Why the key was hidden so firmly, and what lock it fitted, is unknown. Nor is it entirely clear what this had to do with the two mysterious strangers.

One theory holds that these strange events are linked to the second phantom of the pub. This is the ghost of a miner from the 19th century, when several mines were located in the area. As the only public building with a large room, the King's Arms was the site of any inquiries or hearings that needed to be held.

One day a hearing into an accident at a local mine, in which a miner had died, was held here. The magistrate holding the inquiry was of the opinion that he was not getting to the bottom of what had clearly been a strange and dark event. Shortly after the inquiry, one of the miner witnesses, who had given such obviously mis-leading evidence, died. Soon his ghost was seen walking from the mine to the pub, vanishing the instant he reached the door. It was widely presumed that the phantom was trying to deliver the truthful evidence that the poor man had not given in life, his conscience having got the better of him. But he was far too late. The inquiry was over, and the ghost never speaks.

Very definitely able to speak is the shrieking shade which haunts the steep lane outside the pub. Back in late Victorian times, a local woman was

The black monk of Monkton Farleigh was bent over his desk writing when he suffered sudden and unexplained death.

driving home in her light carriage when the horse bolted. Galloping at a terrifying pace, the horse sped down the lane, causing the distraught lady to scream as her carriage bounced and careered dangerously. At the King's Arms one wheel caught the solid stonework of the pub wall, shattering instantly and hurling the doomed woman to her death. More than one person has been startled, on leaving the pub, to hear the ear-piercing scream of a woman in mortal terror. But there is nobody there, and no woman is in trouble. It is merely the ghost from that long-past road accident.

Much more peaceful is the black monk. As the name of the village would suggest, this manor was once the property of a monastery. The monks did not actually live here, but they owned the land, collected the rents, and supervised the community. The King's Arms itself was erected by the monks as the local building where they could do their paperwork, sort out any local disputes, and generally manage the lucrative estates. The oldest part of the building dates back to around 1090, though most of it is some four centuries younger. Not far away was a spring of pure water, which the monks blessed and pronounced to be holy. They constructed a small stone shelter over the spring and sanctified it again.

Then a monk was found dead, slumped over his accounts in what is now the bar of the King's Arms. At the time, foul play was not suspected, and the brethren came and took the body of their companion away for burial. But they could not take away his ghost. Unlike the miner, who walks to the pub, the black monk walks away from it. He makes his way to the small building at the spring, pushes open the door, and then vanishes. What strange mission he might be on is unknown.

Nor is it entirely clear why the black monk gets blamed for the various odd things that go on around the pub. 'We have glasses jump off the shelves, sometimes,' remarked Maria. 'Stuff like that. And things get moved around. When you know you put them in one place, they turn up in another. It's right annoying.'

SEEND

The village of Seend straggles along the A361 between Devizes and Trowbridge. It is a busy road, which carries cars, vans, and trucks that thunder through the village day and night. It is not a road conducive to ghosts, which might be why the ghosts that process through the village have not been seen on the main road much in recent years.

The phantom procession always used to, and still does, make its way to the parish church, and, although the traffic on the main road seems to have blocked its appearances there, the last section of its route is still haunted by the rustic parade. The lane that runs from the A361 to the church is some 200 yards long and is flanked on both sides by high stone walls that cut it off from the grounds of neighbouring grand houses. This is a secluded, almost lonely, spot. The lane ends in a pair of tall ornate gates and an arch of wrought iron. It is here that the ghosts vanish.

The lane at Seend where a whole procession of ghosts has been seen.

One old book records that the ghostly procession is a funeral making its way to the church. A witness who recently saw the ghosts one evening disagrees. 'There were about 20 people coming down the lane towards me,' the witness said. 'I was leaving the church to go home. It was early evening. I thought it odd that so many people would be coming to the church at that time. They were dressed in old-fashioned clothes, which is why I noticed them, but otherwise they looked perfectly normal. I looked down to get something from my handbag, and, when I looked up, they had gone. There was nowhere along that lane they could have gone to; so they were the ghosts, for certain.' Had there been a hearse or coffin? 'No nothing like that. They all seemed quite cheerful, in fact. Chatting to each other and stuff, you know. I couldn't hear what they were saying; they were too far away for that. In fact, now I come to think about it, I'm not sure I heard anything at all.'

Just how ancient the old-fashioned clothing might be is another feature of the hauntings that seems rather obscure. Descriptions say that the ghosts are dressed in the smocks, loose gowns, and wide-brimmed hats that characterized rural day-dress for some centuries before modern, mass-produced clothing put fashion in the purchasing range of almost everyone. Perhaps the phantoms are a century old, perhaps three centuries. However old they might be, the ghosts of Seend are most certainly persistent.

DEVIZES

'Ah well, now then,' said the receptionist at the Wiltshire Heritage Museum. 'I'm not sure we like to publicize that sort of thing any more.' And she proceeded not to publicize them at all.

Staff from previous years were not so reserved. They tell of the figure of an elderly woman in a straw hat who flits quietly around the lower floors of the museum in Long Street. There is no doubt at all as to who this ghost is. She is the phantom of Maud Cunnington, in her time the foremost archaeologist of the county and the only woman to be elected Chairman of the Wiltshire Archaeology and Natural History Society, which runs the museum.

The Cunnington family were for many years the leading figures in the antiquarian and archaeological circles of Wiltshire. It was the Cunningtons who in 1925 excavated the site now known as Woodhenge. Discovered in a field near Durrington, Woodhenge was a site every bit as large and imposing as the rather better-known Stonehenge. The excavation was prompted by the then new-fangled invention of the aeroplane. A pilot flying over the area noticed a series of round marks in the field arranged in what seemed to be concentric circles. The excavation revealed these to be post holes dating back about 4,000 years. They were all that was left of a vast wooden hall, about 140 feet across, which seemed to have had an open courtyard at its centre.

The reports on this and other archaeological digs were written up on a family desk which was made in around 1880. It is this desk that seems to be the centre for the ghostly activity. Perhaps it is the focus for treasured memories.

While the staff are no longer willing to publicize the phantom, they are happy to talk about the impressive range of exhibits and archives at the museum. And impressive they certainly are. There are exhibits from the Bronze Age, in particular the famous Stonehenge urn, one of the first finds of a complete prehistoric cup, which has helped generations of archaeologists to date their discoveries. There is a wide collection of Roman items, including an incense burner shaped like a cockerel and a statue of the god Vulcan. Other

The museum at Devizes, where staff prefer not to talk about ghostly goings-on.

exhibits and displays trace the history of the county down to the present day.

Devizes grew up as a market town sheltering beneath the walls of the castle, which was established in the wake of the Norman Conquest. The castle was intended to overawe any locals who might not have taken too kindly to Norman rule. It has been renovated, altered, rebuilt and remodelled so often over the centuries that virtually nothing of the original remains. Most of the damage was done during the English Civil War, when the owners declared for King Charles I and their stronghold was pounded by Cromwell's cannon as a result. Most of what stands today is barely 150 years old. Despite all the alterations, however, the various ghosts remain.

The oldest of them is the White Lady, who walks sadly up and down the corridors. This phantom is said to be Lady Isabella, daughter of Charles VI of France and wife of Richard II of England. The marriage, celebrated in 1396, was a political one with no love on either side. Richard had made peace in

The court of King Richard II. Queen Isabella, whose phantom allegedly haunts Devizes Castle, sits on his left.

Ireland, and, with this second marriage, made peace with France. It seemed a good deal to Richard, and, no doubt, it appeared a good one to Charles. The girl, Isabella, was not consulted.

In the event, the marriage proved unhappy, both personally and politically. Richard had wanted peace only so that he could cause trouble at home. He believed that some of his nobles, including the Earl of Gloucester, his uncle, were getting too powerful for their own good. A year after the wedding with Isabella, Richard had Gloucester murdered and threw other earls and nobles into prison without trial. He then dismissed Parliament and imposed a host of new taxes that angered his subjects. By 1399, the nobles and people of England had had enough. After the Duke of Hereford had been exiled and dispossessed by Richard based on the flimsiest of evidence, he returned and raised a rebellion. Richard fled to Wales, but was dragged back to London, where he was kept in prison for some months before he conveniently died.

Through all this, the young Isabella was left on her own. According to local legend, she spent her time in Devizes Castle. There she met and became fond of a dashing young man from the local gentry. The friendship grew to love and the liaison blossomed. This could not be tolerated by her husband, who ordered the poisoning of the young knight and had his errant wife walled up alive in the thick fortifications of Devizes Castle. It is this hapless and unfortunate queen of England who is now the beautiful White Lady who paces the corridors of Devizes Castle in search of the happiness she once found there.

Unfortunately, the story cannot possibly be true. Queen Isabella is highly unlikely to have fallen in love with a handsome knight of Devizes, since she was just 6 years old when she was married. Nor can the romantic episode and tragic sequel have happened during the lady's widowhood; she was very much alive when she returned to France at the age of 11. The true identity of the White Lady of Devizes must be said to be unknown.

Equally mysterious is the cavalier who runs down the main staircase in the hall of the castle. This tall and imposing figure hurries down the stairs with much clattering of his boots and with a sword swinging from his belt. He wears a full beard and moustache and has long, flowing locks of hair that cascade down from beneath his hat, but no one knows who he is.

There is at least no doubt about the male voice that mutters at night in one of the upstairs bedrooms of the castle. This is the phantom of a soldier of the Wiltshire Regiment, which used the castle as overflow barracks during the Second World War. One of the men was most unpopular with his messmates, as he not only sleepwalked, but sleeptalked as well. In desperation they gave him a room to himself at night, locked the door, and let him get on with it. It is the room where the man slept that is now plagued by spectral muttering at night.

The most active of the ghosts in the castle is seemingly the least offensive, but there is still something unsettling about her. This is the ghost of an elderly woman dressed in 19th-century widow's weeds, who potters about the upstairs gallery. She uses a walking stick and moves slowly around as if gently passing the time. The dogs of the family do not like this ghost. They flee if she appears. Even when the ghost is not present, the dogs are wary of entering the gallery. Sometimes they will sit at one end of the room watching with great attention and some hostility as something invisible to humans moves around.

ROUNDWAY DOWN

In July 1643, war came to Wiltshire in all its savagery and ferocity. The greatest clash of the campaign took place on the windy hills of Roundway Down outside Devizes. For some of the unfortunate combatants, the fighting continues to this day.

On 5th July 1643, a Parliamentarian general, Sir William Waller, led his army of 4,000 men out of Bath to fight a royalist army under Sir Ralph Hopton, which, although slightly larger, was desperately short of ammunition. The battle was an indecisive affair, but the royalists were running short of food as well as ammunition so they fell back on Devizes, where they hoped to find supplies and reinforcements. Hopton found neither. Waller advanced, eager to press his advantage on the hungry and dispirited royalists. No sooner had Waller reconnoitered the temporary and haphazard defences thrown up around the town by Hopton than the royalist reinforcements came into view.

These were 2,000 cavalry under Lord Wilmot. Waller hurriedly repositioned his 3,000 infantrymen to face the new danger, putting his eight cannon in the centre and 2,000 cavalry on the flanks.

One of the Parliamentarian infantry regiments had men out foraging for firewood when the royalist cavalry rode into sight. These men failed to get back to Waller's main army in time and were charged by the cavaliers. Waller sent forward a force of heavy cavalry to rescue the infantry but they in their turn were defeated and fled.

Wilmot did not hesitate. Ordering his men not to fire their pistols until they were at point blank range, he led his men straight at the Parliamentarian army, which outnumbered his men by two to one. Waller's men fired first, but, at a range of over 75 yards, the primitive muskets of the time did little damage. Wilmot's cavalry reached the Parliamentarians before they had time to reload and fired at a range of less than 5 yards. That first volley was enough. Waller's men began edging backwards. When Hopton marched his men out of Devizes, the Parliamentarians fled.

The Battle of Roundway Down effectively spelt the end of Parliamentarian power in the West Country. Hopton and Wilmot quickly broke up any attempt by Waller to rally his men; then they moved on to capture those towns which had declared for Parliament. In August, the wealthy and strategic city of Bristol fell to Prince Rupert. The king was on the verge of winning the civil war.

That he was later to lose was due largely to the lessons learned by the Parliamentarians at Roundway Down. Discipline was more important than courage alone. It was a lesson learned above all by Oliver Cromwell, a fenland farmer from East Anglia, who would raise and organize the New Model Army, with which he would later sweep through the West Country with devastating effect. This later campaign would leave its ghostly mark at Old Wardour Castle and at Broad Hinton.

Meanwhile, the surprise royalist victory at Roundway Down has its ghosts. As the Roundheads fled, they ran to the west. About 300 yards from the battlefield itself, the rolling upland of Roundway Down ends in an abrupt and frighteningly steep precipice. The fleeing horsemen reached this drop first. Riding at full gallop, many of them plunged over the edge to lose control on the

*The open grassland of Roundway Down, where dramatic ghosts
can appear from nowhere.*

steep slope and be killed in the fall. At the site mass graves have been found
containing the bodies of over 200 men and horses tumbled together. It is on the
land across which they fled that the ghosts are seen. Mounted on wild-eyed
chargers, the phantom Parliamentarian cavalry gallop with frenzied haste as they
seek to escape the swords of the pursuing cavaliers. Time after time, the
frightened men race across the soft downland towards their hideous fate.
Sometimes they are only heard, the noise of pounding hooves and screaming men
sounding quite clearly for a space of several seconds before it is suddenly cut off.

One of the most otherworldly sightings came in the 1970s when a mist sat
on the downs, as it sometimes does on the hills around Devizes. A couple who
were there at the time said that out of this mist came galloping the ghosts of
Roundway Down, looking for all the world like real horsemen plunging into
view and then pounding on to disappear into the mist again. No wonder the

couple who saw them were unnerved by such a strange and sudden apparition, but their experience left them with a fine story to tell.

LACOCK

idely known as one of the most beautiful villages in England, Lacock lives up to its reputation. Most of the village dates from the 15th to 18th centuries, with only enough more recent development to keep the place lively in our modern age. Most of the village is owned by the National Trust, which cares for the fabric of the buildings and the integrity of the general appearance of the place.

The ghosts, for there are more than one, are well scattered in the village. Perhaps the most active is that which haunts Lacock Abbey. As the building's name suggests, the abbey has its origins as a medieval religious house. In this

The beautiful old house of Lacock Abbey, where a deformed dwarf has been seen by several witnesses.

case, it was Augustinian nuns who founded a retreat here in 1232. The establishment achieved both spiritual and financial success, which found expression in magnificent 13th-century cloisters and a fine 15th-century chapter house. When Henry VIII broke up the monasteries in the 16th century and sold their lands and assets, Lacock Abbey was purchased by Sir William Sharington, the Treasurer of the Mint. He retained the cloisters and chapter house, but pulled down the main church to build the magnificent Tudor mansion which stands to this day. In the 19th century, the building was altered somewhat. The most famous local event of the 19th century came in August 1835, when William Fox Talbot pointed an odd looking box at the oriel window of the hall and succeeded in taking the world's first photograph. A museum dedicated to Talbot and his work occupies part of the abbey.

The downstairs corridor of the Angel, haunted by a previous owner of this lovely old inn at Lacock

Given the long history of the abbey it is not surprising that the place is haunted, though to which period its ghost belongs is unknown. The phantom in question is that of a hunchbacked dwarf who scurries hurriedly through the upstairs rooms of the Tudor mansion. He is dressed in dark clothes, but that is about all witnesses can say, for sightings of this ghost are fleeting.

Rather more is known about the beautiful lady who walks gently along the shores of the lake which lies near the abbey. Dressed in a flowing white gown which shifts gently in a soft breeze, regardless of the actual weather at the time, the elegant young woman strolls slowly around the waters. This, the local story goes, is the famed beauty Rosamund Clifford. Her given name, it is said, means 'rose of the world' and was bestowed on her by King Henry II, who was totally besotted with her and took her as mistress after falling out with his haughty queen, Eleanor of Aquitaine.

Young Rosamund was the daughter of the powerful marcher Walter Clifford, who ruled the lands around the Wye Valley with an iron hand. Apart from her stunning beauty and charming manner, very little is known for certain about the fair Rosamund. She died in about 1176, and later generations blamed her death on the jealousy of Eleanor, but there was no such talk at the time. Why this young lady should haunt the lake at Lacock is unknown, but it may be that this was a favoured retreat. There again, this phantom might be the ghost of some other attractive young woman entirely, and the Rosamund connection may be merely a legend.

The Lacock Nun.

In the village high street stands a fine 15th-century structure. Built as a wool merchant's home and subsequently converted into an inn called The Angel, this is now a restaurant. The downstairs is the haunt of a gentle phantom, who causes nobody any trouble at all, though she did once send a carpet fitter fleeing when she appeared suddenly in front of his eyes. This ghost is that of an elderly woman and is thought to be the spectre of the early 20th-century owner of the inn, who cannot bear to leave.

The open country near Lacock also has its share of ghosts. Standing a mile or so outside the village is the 14th-century manor of Bewley Court. The fields between the abbey and the court are said to be haunted by a phantom nun. She has a tragic story. It is thought that as a young girl, she was put into the religious order by her family to fulfil a vow made by her father. As the girl grew older, she became disillusioned with her vocation and longed for a normal family life. In time, she met and fell in love with the son of the family at Bewley Court. The two would tryst down by the river that divided the two estates. Sadly, her sins were discovered, and she was incarcerated in a damp cell at the abbey, where she took sick and died. Now her ghost wanders down to the river where she found some fleeting moments of love and happiness in her earthly life.

Beyond Bewley Court, lie the open lands of Bewley Common. Across this grassland drives a carriage drawn by four horses. It follows neither road nor path, but trots across grass and through trees as if following some long forgotten route all its own.

CORSHAM

The little town of Corsham is perhaps best known for Corsham Court, a magnificent Elizabethan mansion built in 1582 and surrounded by extensive grounds landscaped by Capability Brown in the 18th century. It is not here, however, that ghosts walk.

It is in the rather mundane surroundings of the Corsham Tourist Information Centre that the town's most active phantom resident is to be found. This is the ghost of Miss Pictor, whose home this was from 1936 to 1959. Miss Pictor was the last of the famous Pictor family which earned a vast fortune from quarrying the local building stone. Miss Pictor long had a reputation as a miser. Everyone knew she was wealthy, but she never spent much money and habitually wore old, worn-out clothes. She would sit at an upstairs window in the house, watching the inhabitants of Corsham going about their business. After she died, Miss Pictor was found to have left her expected vast fortune to distant relatives.

Then her ghost began to walk. 'Oh yes, old Miss Pictor,' confirmed the man on duty at the information centre in late 2003. 'She comes through that doorway there,' he said, pointing to the downstairs corridor and a doorway to the right of the front door. 'We've got an electronic counter thing that is supposed to tell us how many people come in and out of the information centre, but it counts her as well. Sometimes it goes off even when you don't see the ghost. But we know she is there anyway.' Another member of staff confirmed the presence of the ghost: 'We first noticed the strange noises a few years ago, just after we opened. It is like footsteps from the room upstairs,' this being the room from which Miss Pictor would watch

The stone set into the wall of the Tourist Information Centre records the generosity of the woman who now haunts it.

passers-by and the various goings-on of Corsham. 'You hear more things when you are in here alone. Perhaps customers frighten her off. And lightbulbs are always blowing, and being switched off.'

In October 2003, BBC Radio Wiltshire sent an outside broadcast team to the site to do a feature on the ghost. The team was led by the appropriately named Heather Skull, while the anchor man back at the studios, James Harrison, helpfully put a sheet over his head and shouted 'boo' from time to time to get everyone in the mood. Miss Pictor did not put in an appearance, but it was a jolly radio show, nonetheless.

There are other ghosts in Corsham, but they do not seem to be seen as often as Miss Pictor and have certainly not been the focus of a radio show. The church of St Bartholomew has a rather odd and most unpleasant ghost. The church itself dates back to Norman times, but much of the present building is the result of a major reconstruction in the 19th century.

The best recorded sighting of the ghost came in the 1930s, when Lady Winifred Pennoyer and a friend were sitting in the churchyard and chatting. Walking between the tombstones, came a very short and rather stocky man. As he came close to the two women, he turned and gave them a stare of undiluted hatred and evil. Lady Winifred was severely shocked by the utter malevolence she felt emanating from the man. She turned to her friend, only to find that she had fainted and was now unconscious. The man promptly vanished. When the friend came to, she reported seeing the little man and then being overwhelmed by fear and dread, after which she remembered nothing. The hideous little man is not seen very often, which is probably just as well. Those who do see him usually report feelings which vary from unease to downright hostility – a strange phantom, and one best avoided.

Rather more mainstream is the ghost which stalks along the little street known as Monk's Park. Common sense would indicate this ghost should be a monk, but it is not. The phantom seen here is described as being a Roman legionary. He wears steel armour and a short, skirt-like affair studded with metal plates. Although this phantom does not carry the typical oblong Roman shield, he otherwise fits the description of a Roman soldier. What he is doing in Monk's Park is altogether unclear.

The final ghost of Corsham is larger, louder, and more spectacular than all the others. Indeed, it is just possibly the most impressive in all Wiltshire. Corsham lies on what was the Great Western Railway, built by that great Victorian engineer, Isambard Kingdom Brunel. Just west of Corsham the route of the London–Bristol rail line was interrupted by a range of hills. Brunel decided to drive a tunnel straight through these hills, and the result was the mighty Box Tunnel. Time was of the essence, so Brunel set 4,000 men to work, hacking a way through the rock with pickaxe and shovel. The two-mile tunnel was completed on time, though local legend has it that it cost the lives of 100 men.

It is not these labourers who haunt the railway between Corsham and the Box Tunnel, but a railway train. Painted in the bold colours of the Great Western Railway, this steam train of 1920s' vintage comes tearing out of the tunnel at high speed. Smoke billows from the funnel, steam spurts from the pistons, and the wheels spin with whirling speed. Rushing along as if every moment counts, the train pounds the line for almost a mile until it reaches the outskirts of Corsham. There it fades from view. 'Imagine you put a stone in water and let it drop,' said one witness. 'At first you see it very clearly. Then it seems to fade and get a bit blurry. Then it is gone.'

KILMINGTON

The otherwise peaceful village of Kilmington was shocked by the news of what happened in the churchyard one day in 1555. The local landowner, the 8th Baron Stourton, had long had a reputation for violent behaviour and a quick temper. Both came into play that day and they were to cost more than one life and result in more than one ghost.

The chain of events that led up to the fatal day, and to the hauntings that followed, began in 1551, when the 7th Baron Stourton, William, died. The Stourtons, though not of the highest nobility, were well connected and wealthy. Baron William's wife was Lady Elizabeth Dudley, the daughter of Edmund Dudley, Duke of Northumberland. It was Lady Elizabeth who had brought most of the wealth to the family and, now her husband was dead, it reverted to her. Only on her death would her estates pass to her son, the new Baron Stourton.

But the new baron, Charles, was in a hurry. He had debts to pay and a life of debauchery to lead. Just a few weeks after his father's death, young Charles rode to Kilmington to see his mother. Using the pretence that the family assets should all be kept under one control, he demanded that his mother hand over her jewels, gold, and the title deeds of her property at once. The old lady was on the point of doing so, when she was interrupted by William Hartgill, the steward of her estates. Hartgill suggested that Charles should give his mother an annuity to live on. The two men quarrelled violently, and Charles stormed out without his mother's wealth.

The following Sunday – Whit Sunday – Lord Charles Stourton hired a gang of twenty toughs and lay in wait at the church in Kilmington for the Hartgills to arrive for Sunday service. Fortunately for the Hartgills, their son John was planning to go hunting with friends after the service and had with him his

The church tower at Kilmington, where a bloody fight led to murder.

bow and a crossbow. As the Hartgills approached the church, Stourton and his men charged with swords drawn. Young John dropped one man with his bow and then led his parents into the church, where they barricaded themselves in the tower. The Hartgills managed to fight off Stourton and his men until the forces of law and order arrived in the person of Sir Thomas Speak, High Sheriff of Somerset.

The courts threw Lord Stourton in prison and ordered him to pay compensation to his victims, which he flatly refused to do. In 1555, he was released and he returned to his home, but he had neither forgiven nor forgotten his imagined grievances. At Christmas, Stourton sent a message to the Hartgills offering to meet them at the church, to pay the compensation for the injuries he had caused them, and to use the season of goodwill to end the feud.

The Hartgills were understandably suspicious and arranged for several local gentlemen to be at the church on the day set for the meeting. All seemed to go well, Stourton handed over a purse of coins and pledged friendship. But it was just a ruse to put his quarry off their guard. As divine service ended, the congregation left the church to find themselves under the guns of two dozen men hired by Stourton. Triumphant and full of rage, Stourton ordered the two Hartgill men to be tied up and thrown onto a cart. When Mrs Hartgill protested, Stourton stabbed her. A scuffle broke out, but Stourton had the guns and he got his way. The Hartgills were dragged off and promptly vanished.

A few days later, one of the men Stourton had hired for the treachery at the church went to see the local magistrate, Sir Anthony Hungerford. The man revealed that Stourton had told them he meant to kidnap and beat the Hartgills, but in fact they had been murdered. The man showed Sir Anthony where the bodies were hidden and then quickly fled the area. Hungerford moved promptly, arresting Stourton and four of his men that night. A search of the Stourton home found not only clear evidence of the murder, but also stolen cattle and sheep, together with the proceeds of a local robbery.

Because of his aristocratic connections, Stourton was taken to London for trial. Found guilty, he was returned to Wiltshire for execution. He was hanged in Salisbury Market Place on 6 March 1557 and buried in the cathedral, where his tomb became the centre of some paranormal activity. The four men who had helped Stourton in the murder were hanged at Kilmington.

These dramatic events, played out in a quiet churchyard, have left their spectral mark. The two ghosts seen most often are those of the two Hartgills. Father and son walk solemnly around the church as if deep in discussion. Also seen, though rarely, is a man armed with a gun and sword. Rather more sinister, this figure hides among the shrubs and trees, keeping to the shadows, and is not seen clearly. Presumably he is one of the murderers.

Once Lord Charles Stourton was dispatched by justice, Kilmington returned to its peaceful ways. The Stourton's titles and estates passed to Charles's eldest son, John. To everyone's enormous relief, John had inherited neither his father's temper nor his taste for violence. So far as is known, deadly treachery has never again marred this village.

ZEALS HOUSE

The haunting at Zeals House, just yards inside the Wiltshire border, began with a mystery and ended with a tragedy. Back in the 18th century, the daughter of the house began a romance with a servant from the village of Zeals. Needless to say, her father disapproved, not only as the young man was very definitely from the wrong

The gates to Zeals House, now a private residence, but public footpaths cross the haunted fields and woods.

class, but also because he was a rather shady character who had drifted into the village from nobody quite knew where. Despite all the father could do, however, his wayward daughter found ways to see her beloved.

One morning, Zeals House woke up to find the girl gone. She had taken with her a trunk of clothes and her jewellery, along with a pot of gold her father kept in the house for paying tradesmen and the like. Gone also was the servant from the village. It was presumed the pair had eloped. Riders were sent out far and wide to track down a young couple on the run, but there was no sign of the runaways. After some weeks, the family gave up hope of tracking down their daughter and just prayed that one day she would make contact – which was when the ghost began to walk.

Dressed in a long grey cloak, the daughter of the house was seen to walk down the stairs and slip out of a door. Walking across the grounds, the girl skirted the lake and vanished into the woods beyond. Glimpsed at first by servants too frightened to talk of what they had seen, the ghost appeared less frequently as time passed. Word of the apparition reached the family, and, fearing the worst, they searched the woods but found nothing.

In the 1890s, however, a skeleton was found in a shallow grave on the edge of a field on the far side of the woods. There were, of course, no jewels and no gold. It would seem that the poor girl had been duped by a villain who murdered her for the money he could grab.

Once the bones had received a proper burial, the ghost walked less often. However, folk say that she is still sometimes seen flitting about the field where her bones were found and where, it is presumed, she was brutally murdered.

A350, TWO MILE DOWN

The ghost of Two Mile Down is one of those enigmatic phantoms which is often seen, but to which no story or legend is attached. The spectre, which appears here with some regularity, is of a coach drawn by four grey horses. The coach is closed, so it is impossible to see the passengers, if there are any. The coachman does not attract much attention from those who see this spectre; none of the witnesses has given a clear description of him. Presumably, therefore, he is not headless or missing, as either would surely be noticed.

Whether the coach is linked to some great tragedy or romance, nobody seems to know. All that can be said with certainty is that a Victorian coach-and-four returns in spectral form to ride down the main road across Two Mile Down – for reasons of its own.

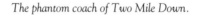

The phantom coach of Two Mile Down.

WINKLEBURY CAMP

Towering above the village of Berwick St John, the ancient Iron Age hillfort of Winklebury Camp defied the Romans and saw action in the Anglo and Saxon invasions four centuries later. It is not, however, these bloody days gone by that have left their supernatural mark here, but something altogether more sinister, evil, and dangerous.

For some reason the Devil has made Winklebury Camp his own. Not that he is to be found here all the time, of course. One must assume that the Devil is busy in many parts of this wicked old world every day of the year. But he can be summoned to Winklebury Camp – and very easily. All that is needed is for a brave soul to climb this steep hill after dark, find the ancient earthwork fortifications, and run around them seven times.

The Devil himself will then appear, mounted on a terrifying horse with a jet black coat. Having been thus summoned, the Devil is bound to grant one wish to the person who has called him.

The commanding heights of Winklebury, where evil can be summoned up all too easily.

The task is not so easy as it might sound, on two counts. First, the circuit of the fortifications is more than half a mile over broken ground; so running round them seven times in the dark would be rather tricky. More worryingly, you can never be certain that you will get what you want when you bargain with the Devil. He is all too prone to fulfil the letter of his promise, and then to trick the misguided folk, who summoned him into giving away their soul, or that of someone close to them.

It is probably best, all things considered, to avoid Winklebury Camp.

WARDOUR CASTLE

One of the most charming ruins in Wiltshire is that of Old Wardour Castle, which stands in the grounds of New Wardour Castle, a grand manor house. Although the new castle is private, the old castle is open to the public. It is not well signposted, however, and can only be found by turning off the A30 at Donhead St Andrew and following signs to Ansty. The castle is signposted off this road to the right.

Unfortunately for those living there at the time, Wardour Castle was all too easy to find when Oliver Cromwell and his Roundheads came marching through Wiltshire during the English Civil War of the 1640s. The castle had been built in 1393 for John, Lord Lovel, as a stronghold to protect his estates. In the years that followed, Wardour Castle was maintained more as a luxury home than a fortress and by the 17th century the fortifications were hopelessly out of date. Nevertheless, its owner, Lady Blanche Arundell, refused to surrender her home when Cromwell called.

Lady Blanche was aged 60 at the time and was a staunch royalist, as was her husband, Baron Thomas. In 1643, the baron was riding with the king's army along with those young men from his estates who had followed the drum. So Lady Blanche had only 25 male servants on whom to call for help when Cromwell arrived. The gates of Wardour Castle were slammed shut and the barrels of ammunition broken open. Armed with just muskets and swords, the 'garrison' defied Cromwell to do his worst, which is exactly what he did.

Bringing up heavy cannon, the Roundheads proceeded to pound Wardour Castle. The ancient stone walls stood up well, but in the end they could not resist the constant battering by heavy iron balls. After two weeks, the luxurious apartments had been destroyed and a gaping breach opened in the defensive walls. Without hope, Lady Blanche surrendered. Her garrison was let go, and she was hauled off to a Parliamentarian prison, where she was to die a few months later after hearing that her beloved husband had been killed in battle.

Not long afterwards, the wraith of Lady Blanche began to be seen on the Wardour estates. To this day she wanders around the ruins of her old home and is often seen down by the extensive lake which laps at the northern walls of the castle. Those who have seen her say the ghost walks with small but dignified steps. The phantom is dressed in a long cloak, though whether it is grey or brown is uncertain. She is most often seen at twilight, moving silently and slowly as she tours her old estates.

Wardour Castle, once the scene of brutal fighting, but now a peaceful ruin.

Although both Lady Blanche and Baron Thomas were dead, they had a son, who now became Baron Henry of Wardour. Young Henry was as bold a supporter of the king as his parents. Gathering his men, he rode to Wardour Castle and with great bravery entered while the Roundhead garrison was still repairing the walls. Packing the Parliamentarians off to prison in their turn, Baron Henry now held the castle.

King Charles I was, however, doomed to lose the civil war and to be executed. Sadly, Baron Henry sailed into exile as an impoverished man. More fortunately, his experience in war made him much in demand among the armies of Europe, where he earned a living for some years. On his travels, Baron Thomas met the exiled King Charles II, who was a few years his junior, and the two men got along well. When Charles regained his throne in 1660, Baron Henry came back to England with him.

Baron Henry was restored to his estates and was, ever after, one of the new king's companions. He found his home a neglected ruin and set about building

The lake below Wardour Castle, where a quiet phantom walks.

a new seat for his family, leaving the old ruin to be enjoyed by his mother's phantom.

WOODMINTON

The village of Woodminton is scarcely a hamlet, consisting of just a scattering of houses without benefit of church, shop, or pub. It lies in the valley of the Ebbe, where the precipitous slopes of the hills to the south drop down into the valley floor. This narrow area is quiet now, but it was once a key location.

The Roman invasion of Britain was in its second phase when the legions came to Woodminton, or whatever the place was then named. The tribes of the south-east had been subdued in AD 43; now the Romans were driving west to reach the easily defended Severn–Trent line, where they planned to halt their conquests.

The rich lands of Wiltshire were then in the hands of the Atrebates, a warlike tribe of Celts who lacked nothing in courage. At first the Atrebates, under their king, Tincommius, welcomed the Roman invasion as it led to the destruction of their old tribal enemies, the Catuvellauni, who ruled the lower Thames valley. By AD 47, however, the true purpose of the Romans had become clear, and the proud Atrebates were unwilling to become merely another subject-people paying taxes to Rome.

At this point one of the greatest figures of early British history strode into the unhappy villages of the Atrebates. This was King Caractacus. Charismatic, popular, and one of the most skilled warriors of the Celtic world, Caractacus believed that the tribes of Britain had to join forces to drive out the Romans. His skills lay in hit-and-run raids, ambushes, and fast movements which left the heavily armoured Roman legionaries bemused. A set-piece battle with the Romans would almost certainly be lost, Caractacus believed, but a long campaign of attrition might sap the will of Rome to conquer Britain.

Although he was from the Catuvellauni tribe, Caractacus found a willing audience among the warriors of the Atrebates. When the Roman XX Valeria

Legion came to attack the Atrebates, Caractacus laid one of his famous ambushes. The spot chosen for the attack was Woodminton. The Romans were marching west up the valley of the Ebbe towards what is now called Winklebury Camp, then one of the strongholds of the Atrebates. The Romans had overrun many of these earth and timber strongholds before. Despite Winklebury's great height and steep slopes, the Romans would have been confident of success. They did not count on being ambushed before they even got there. At Woodminton the Celtic warriors pounced. Using the steep slope to their advantage, they poured down to smash the Roman column on its flank.

It is this scene that is recreated in spectral form at Woodminton on nights when the moon is bright. Sometimes only the sounds of battle are heard: clashing swords, screams, and pounding hooves. But on rare occasions the full battle is to be seen played out on the fields around Woodminton. The legions

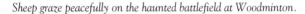

Sheep graze peacefully on the haunted battlefield at Woodminton.

march with their customary discipline and measured tramp, while the Celts dash forwards with individual bravery and wild fervour. Their bodies painted in sacred designs and their hair spiked up with mud and brightly coloured, these Celts make a terrifying sight.

The ambush at Woodminton proved to be just one clash in a war that would continue for almost a decade. The superior resources of Rome eventually ground down the British tribes. Caractacus himself was captured and hauled off to Rome. He was paraded through the streets of the city in front of the triumphal chariot of the Emperor Claudius. Asked if he had anything to say before being executed, Caractacus gestured at Rome's marble temples and sumptuous palaces. 'If you have all this,' he asked 'why did you want my wooden hut?' Claudius spared Caractacus's life and he was kept in comfortable house imprisonment in Italy to the end of his days.

The British warrior King Caractacus is dragged before the Roman Emperor Claudius after his capture.

BOWERCHALKE

The small village of Bowerchalke hides an old legend and, just possibly, a remarkable treasure. The village itself is one of the more attractive in the area, strung out along the lane which runs at the foot of the steep chalk hills to the south. Along the base of these hills rises a series of springs, the waters of which join to form a stream. Over this stream crosses the Applespill Bridge, which is where the first of the phantoms is to be seen.

The ghosts of Applespill Bridge are seven in number. They walk slowly as they carry a coffin on their shoulders over the bridge and towards the church. It might be thought that this is the phantom recreation of a funeral procession of years gone by, but local legends are rather more colourful. According to the old story, one of the prehistoric burial barrows up on the chalk downs was opened many years ago by a gentleman interested in antiquities – there were no such things as archaeologists in those days. Inside the barrow were found the bones of a tall and mighty man, accompanied by a sword, spear and shield. There was also, it is said, a vast store of gold. The only container readily to hand that was large and strong enough to hold the gold was a coffin. The antiquary piled the gold into the coffin and got seven workmen to carry the treasure down into the village. It is the ghostly recreation of this scene that explains the spectres of Applespill Bridge.

Of course, a poetic ending for the legend would have been for those who found the gold to encounter ill fortune or even death. But this appears not to have been the case. Those who plundered the tomb seem to have been able to benefit from the gold stolen from the ancient dead, though why they return in spectral form is unknown.

Less of a mystery is the reason for the return of old Mrs Elliott. This kindly old lady was, in the later 19th century, the local nurse, midwife, and doctor all rolled into one. She had a skill with herbs and a cheery bedside manner which made her much in demand. As was the way with these local healers, old Mrs Elliott did not charge for her services, but she was always given a share of the garden vegetables by those she helped and she could be confident of receiving

The stream at Bowerchalke, which is crossed by a funereal procession.

pies and sausages whenever a local pig was killed.

In time, of course, old Mrs Elliott passed away. Soon afterwards, children in the area who fell ill began reporting that a kindly old lady came to sit with them and held their hands when their parents were not around. No adult ever saw this ghost, so identification was impossible. Nobody was in any doubt, however, that old Mrs Elliott was still ministering to the sick of the parish as she had done when alive. The ghost remained active for over 50 years, but has not been reported since the Second World War.

Still very active is a more plaintive and sad spectre which haunts the hills south of the village. These hills are steep and spectacular, but they are also blasted by high winds and lashed by any bad weather in the area. In summer, when hot sunshine bathes the hills, the constant wind can be bracing, even refreshing. But in winter that same wind is bitter – and dangerous. Many years ago a shepherd up in the hills was gathering his flock to take them down to the valley as the winter weather closed in. A sudden blizzard hit the uplands, taking the poor man entirely by surprise. He lost his way and, after blundering around for some hours, he eventually froze to death. His body was later found and decently buried, but his spirit remains. Clad in an old-time smock, the man wanders around blindly, calling out clearly, if plaintively, 'I want to go home. I want to go home.' Sadly, of course, he never will.

Even sadder is the ghostly girl who sits by the wayside at a crossroads south of the village. This poor girl killed herself in the days when suicide was counted a great sin by the church and those who killed themselves were not allowed to be buried in hallowed ground. Instead they were buried at crossroads. This poor phantom sits on her grave and avoids the eyes of passers-by, always turning her head away, as if ashamed. It would seem Bowerchalke has not always been a happy place.

SALISBURY

The city of Salisbury is one of the most attractive in England and is the only city in Wiltshire. The centre preserves its medieval street plan and has many ancient buildings within it. In recent years the building of modern housing estates outside the centre has boosted the vibrancy of the city without spoiling its old-time charm.

Although the origins of Salisbury go back to pre-Roman times, the current site has been occupied since only around 1220. It was in that year that Bishop Robert Poore pulled down the old cathedral located within the ramparts of the Roman town, Sorviodunum, high on the hills to the north, and began building the current cathedral down in the valley, where the water supply was better and the wind less violent. The people of Salisbury soon followed the bishop's lead and eagerly settled around the cathedral. The ghosts of Salisbury cluster there still.

Indeed, the more enigmatic phantoms are to be found at the cathedral itself. The most dramatic of these are the giant white birds, larger than swans, that fly around the spire to announce the death of the bishop or some other senior cleric associated with the building. The most notorious sighting occurred in 1885. A certain Miss Moberly was walking across the cathedral close when she saw the huge birds wheeling above her. Not knowing of the legend, she pointed out the strange birds to a workman, who told her of the old story. The event was all the more disturbing because Miss Moberly was the daughter of the then bishop, who was grievously ill. The poor girl hurried home, but her father died later that day.

Poultry Cross, the scene of a very modern haunting.

One of the oddest tombs in the county is that of Lord Stourton, who in 1555 was involved in an extraordinary chain of events that ended with him committing a double murder. No one could doubt his lordship's guilt, and death by hanging was the sentence of the court. When Lord Stourton was led into the market place for his execution, he found that the usual rope of hemp had been replaced by one of finest silk. Despite his crimes he was allowed to be buried in the cathedral, and the strange silken cord was suspended over his tomb. In 1780 the dean thought the rope in bad taste and took it down. Despite this, the fatal silken cord – or at least its glowing phantom – has been seen on several occasions.

The double murder led to its own hauntings, as described in the chapter on Kilmington (see page 38).

Away from the cathedral another phantom lurks at the Poultry Cross, which is almost as ancient as the cathedral itself. This market cross of carved stone, the arches of which once provided shelter for market stalls, now serves the same purpose for shoppers and tourists. The ghost here can be difficult to spot. He is a man in a grey, pinstripe three-piece business suit. He stands quietly by himself, but attracts attention by some unidentified oddness about him. Then he vanishes abruptly, like a light being flicked off.

An older ghost in a more modern setting is that of tall, handsome Henry, Duke of Buckingham, who haunts Debenhams department store. The present shop was built in part on what was once the Blue Boar Inn, the rear courtyard of which remains an open space. The boar was the personal emblem of King Richard III, adopted in the days when he was the Duke of Gloucester, the younger brother of heroic King Edward IV, and it is because of Richard III that Buckingham haunts this place.

In 1483, Richard took the throne after the sons of Edward IV had been declared illegitimate. These boys were the famous Princes in the Tower, whose continued existence was something of an embarrassment to both Richard and the monarch who followed him, Henry VII. Which king had them murdered is unknown, though they were undoubtedly killed. However, Richard did not need to murder the Duke of Buckingham; he had him tried and legally executed instead. In his coup, Richard had been helped by Buckingham, one of England's wealthiest men and a cousin of Edward and Richard. Within weeks of Richard coming to

A tall, handsome ghost lurks inside Debenhams, while a playful spectre haunts the street outside.

power, Buckingham changed his mind; with royal blood in his veins, he thought he had as much right to rule as Richard. He sent out messages calling on his men to arm themselves for war and to meet him at Bristol. The duke rode west, but a sudden and terrible storm caused widespread floods across the West Country. Unable to reach Bristol, Buckingham was caught by Richard's men.

The hapless duke was taken to Salisbury for trial. He was lodged in the Blue Boar Inn, as this was the only building which offered rooms both luxurious enough for a duke and secure enough to act as a prison. Found guilty, Buckingham was given the dignity of a private execution and a quick death. He was beheaded in the courtyard of the inn. His headless ghost has been seen standing in the yard and areas nearby. An air of sadness and melancholy is associated with the ghost, though the phantom's emotions are difficult to gauge, as he lacks a head.

Whilst the duke haunts the area to the rear of the store, the street front is said to be haunted by the playful spectre of a little girl. Dressed in Victorian clothes, the girl scampers about with evident glee and happiness. Who she is and why she chooses to haunt this particular street is unknown.

Far better known is the story behind the haunting of the Haunch of Venison pub. This fine old inn was built in 1320 to house the masons and other craftsmen working on the construction of the cathedral spire. It is said that the odd layout of the building, with floors on different levels, reflects the strict hierarchy of the workmen, foremen, and master masons who lived there – the more senior men living on the higher floors. Be that as it may, the lowest and smallest rooms were used by Winston Churchill in the spring of 1944, when he came here to confer with General Dwight Eisenhower over the planning for D-Day. The complex operation of landing thousands of men and hundreds of tanks on the Normandy beaches to begin the defeat of Hitler's Germany required both military precision and political skills. These rooms provided the security for the talks and enough space to lay out the necessary maps.

Nevertheless, the ghosts of the Haunch of Venison owe nothing to workmen or wartime planners. The most active ghost goes by the name of The Demented Whist Player, for nobody knows his real name. The man was travelling through Salisbury in the 1820s and lodged at the Haunch of

Venison. What happened next is probably best told in the words of the poem
which hangs on the walls in the bar.

> He'd travelled all day from Southampton,
> His horse was stabled and fed,
> And he entered the Haunch of Venison
> To see if they'd give him a bed.
>
> The locals were drinking and playing
> At cards and shove-ha'penny too,
> And with one accord they stopped talking
> As the stranger came into view.
>
> Their silence did not deter him;
> He ordered his ale, which he downed,
> Then he tossed a gold coin to the pot boy
> And called 'Ale for all those around.'
>
> Immediately he was accepted,
> Was drawn straight away to their game,
> And though he was lucky a few times
> To him it seemed rustic and tame.
>
> Then suddenly he started winning.
> The silence became quite profound,
> For he'd soon won the price of his lodging
> And five times the cost of his round.
>
> A big butcher, seated quite near him,
> Was growing belligerent, and,
> Drawing his blade from its scabbard,
> He struck off the stranger's right hand.

The man screamed in horror and anguish;
How on earth had the trick been exposed?
For clutched in the hand in the rushes
Five aces were clearly disclosed.

Bizarrely, the mummified hand gripping five faded aces is preserved in a box at the Haunch of Venison. Presumably it serves as a warning to strangers of how the men of Salisbury deal with cheats.

It is said that the vengeful spirit of the man deprived of his hand, cards, and winnings comes back to the pub to exact his revenge. It is this spirit which hides objects, throws open doors, and slams them shut again. A Frenchman who came here to manage the restaurant in 2002 reported that he often found taps, lights and electric switches turned off when he was certain he had left them on, and on when he had left them off. Usually these events were accompanied by a definite smell of freshly turned earth, which is most odd in such an ancient and well-settled building.

The second ghost at the Haunch is a sad and upsetting phantom. This is the ghost of a young lady in a white shawl, which is seen both in the pub and in Minster Street outside. About a century ago, she sent her young son to the pub to purchase a few bottles, but he never returned. Whether the boy was kidnapped, killed for the money he carried, or simply met with an accident has never been discovered. The poor mother, of course, came to the pub to ask after her son, but he had never arrived. Day after day the distraught woman wandered around looking for her child, until she took sick and died. And now her ghost continues the endless search that will never have a happy ending.

LARKHILL

Standing on a remote, windswept corner high on Salisbury Plain is a squat stone cross which commemorates a tragic accident that occurred almost a century ago. The event is also remembered by the ghosts which recreate the fatal crash to this day.

The monument near Larkhill which commemorates Britain's first air crash fatalities.

The corner lies where the A344 meets the B3086, and a short lay-by gives access to the memorial. This cross is dedicated to Captain B. Lorraine and Sergeant R. Wilson, who died here when the aircraft they were flying tumbled from the sky and crashed, in the summer of 1912. These early aircraft were flimsy structures made of light wood and covered with cotton fabric stiffened with dope. Powered by weak engines which were prone to sudden failure, such planes were risky things to fly at the best of times. They were, however, proving to be invaluable for military reconnaissance, and so soldiers such as Lorraine and Wilson were learning to fly.

Nobody really knows what caused the crash, but it seems likely that the wooden frame simply collapsed under the strain of flying. Whatever the cause, the aircraft crashed at this remote spot and both men were killed.

Ever since, the small aircraft has been seen from time to time chugging gently in the sky above this road junction. It then suddenly puts its nose down and crashes to earth. Some who have seen it have feared the worst and either dashed to the site or used their mobile phones to call for assistance from ambulance and police. Any assistance would be almost a century too late; the unfortunate airmen are long since beyond human help.

A pre-First World War British military aircraft of the type that crashed at Larkhill.

BULFORD

The road running north from Bulford has a ghost which indulges in an activity not generally associated with ghosts. He whistles.

The ghost is said to be that of a cavalier and is referred to by the local press as 'The Whistling Cavalier' when a sighting is reported. The reason for this identification is not entirely clear. He certainly wears a hat with a wide brim, but otherwise his clothing seems to be more in keeping with that of a country villager than that of a dashing cavalier. Perhaps his jaunty air and cheerful whistling put people in mind of the painting entitled *The Laughing Cavalier*.

A typical sighting was made in 1995. A teenage girl was out late one summer's night, when: 'I heard the sound of somebody whistling very loudly and very clearly. The tune was "Greensleeves" and the whistler kept repeating the first few bars over and over again. I caught a glimpse of a man in a hat, but he slipped out of sight within a second or two and the whistling soon faded.'

ALLINGTON

Not far from the site of a presumed suicide by a clergyman in Cholderton is the village of Allington, where another cleric came to a premature end and now returns in spectral form. This time, it was the village curate, who had dined very well at the local manor house. When he left the manor, he was the worse for drink and had trouble mounting his horse. The animal turned up alone at home some time later, and the next morning the curate's body was found by the roadside. It was assumed he had fallen from his horse and had broken his neck.

At least, that was the story told at the time by those who had been at the dinner. But it was not long before villagers noticed that the diners were behaving in a strange and furtive manner. When the ghost of the curate began

The village of Allington, where a phantom indicates that a convivial dinner may have hidden a dark, deadly secret.

to be seen, it led to further gossip. The ghost was seen to walk, not ride, from the manor to the spot where the body was found. A few months later, one of those who had been present at the dinner lay dying and called for a vicar. The man was clearly desperate to unburden himself of some great guilt and fretted anxiously in great distress. By the time a clergyman could be brought, however, the man was beyond speech. He died without revealing whatever secret he had tried to tell.

Of those who knew what really happened, only the ghost now remains in Allington. And the ghost is not telling.

CHOLDERTON

In 1896 a visiting clergyman left his bed at Cholderton House one night and went missing. He took with him his dressing gown, but left behind his day clothes, money, and travelling bag. A few days later his body was found at the base of a disused well near the church. The discovery was made when a passer-by noticed the missing man's slippers placed neatly on the parapet of the well.

It was widely assumed at the time that the man had committed suicide. No personal, financial, or family troubles were unearthed to explain the event, but neither was there any sign of foul play. An open verdict was recorded by the coroner and the matter was allowed to rest. At least it was allowed to rest by the living, but not by the dead. Strange noises began to be heard at the well by those who passed by after dark. Soon rumours swept the village that the man had been murdered and his body dumped in the well by persons unknown. It all caused quite a stir in Cholderton, but nothing was ever proved and no credible suspects were ever found.

But the hauntings go on. Some even claim to see the doomed man walking to his death, clad in slippers and dressing gown. Perhaps one day the mystery will be solved, and the restless spirit will be able to take off its slippers and dressing gown and go to a final sleep at last.

• The North •

CASTLE COMBE

T his village is probably the most photographed in Wiltshire. It has featured on more greetings cards and chocolate boxes than perhaps any other in England. The old market cross, with its vaulted stone roof, and the ancient stone houses serve as a perfect backdrop for the babbling By Brook as it tumbles down the narrow valley and under the three-arched bridge at the lower end of the village.

The By Brook flows through Castle Combe and served as a focus for the battle that raged here over a thousand years ago.

Castle Combe owes its charm and beauty to a burst of prosperity in the 16th century, when a group of Flemish weavers came here. They established an industry weaving the local woollen thread into quality cloth, and so brought enough money to this little village to build the bridge, houses and market cross that make it so attractive.

But it is the narrow valley itself that explains the ghosts that lurk here. The steeply wooded slopes that flank the twisting road would make a deadly site for an ambush in any war, and it is the sounds of fighting men hacking at each other with swords, spears and axes that sometimes shatters the quiet calm of the woodlands. There are no guns going off in this phantom battle, nor are there horses' hooves to be heard – just the clash of metal on metal and the screams and cries of men shouting in a guttural language.

This startling manifestation is the faint echo of a small skirmish fought here centuries ago that saved England as a nation. In the 860s England was invaded by a large army of Vikings, led by the mighty warrior Guthrum. These men did not come to raid, but to stay, conquer and settle. They crushed the kingdoms of East Anglia, Northumbria and Mercia in short order. In 871 they turned on Wessex, which then covered most of southern England including Wiltshire. A long series of battles followed, but by 875 King Alfred of Wessex had fought the Vikings to a standstill. Guthrum took oaths to his pagan gods, promising peace, and led his army back to the parts of England they had already conquered.

Alfred set about rebuilding his kingdom after the ravages of war. By Christmas 877, he was well on his way to success and went to the sumptuous royal residence at Chippenham to celebrate the festive season. But Guthrum was biding his time and was determined to crush the last English king, so that the Viking conquest of England would be complete. Believing, correctly, that the Christian feast of Christmas would be a good time to strike, Guthrum led his army on a secret march to Chippenham.

On Twelfth Night, the Vikings struck. Most of Alfred's men were at home on their estates across Wessex, and he had only his personal bodyguard with him. The Viking onrush came at night when many men were drunk, sleeping, or both. A determined rearguard held up the pagans just long enough for

*The dense woods around Castle Combe where the ghosts fight their
never-ending battle for the future of England.*

Alfred to get away and send messengers to those living nearby, asking them to
meet him urgently.

Soon after, Alfred and the few men who had answered his summons met up
somewhere near Chippenham. A force of Vikings had tracked Alfred and were
hard on his heels. The English ambushed the Vikings, driving them off and
giving Alfred time to slip away to hide in the Somerset marshes. In time,
Alfred would muster an army to crush Guthrum's Vikings once and for all. He
would then set about rebuilding Wessex as a powerful state, reconquer much of
Mercia, and lay the foundations for the united kingdom of England that we all
know.

Where the ambush of the Vikings was carried out was not recorded. Given
the ghosts of Castle Combe, however, the site would seem to be established.
Not only is the narrow valley a perfect place for this type of an ambush, but it

is just four miles from Chippenham. A fleeing king could cover such a distance at night, and the valley is as good a place to muster a force in secret as it is to launch an ambush.

If the fighting ghosts of Castle Combe are Alfred's Englishmen driving off the Vikings, then these are most significant ghosts. If this battle had ended differently and Alfred had died, Wiltshire would now be a Scandinavian county, not an English one.

But battling Vikings are not the only phantoms of Castle Combe. Near the village are the crumbling foundations of the eponymous castle, built by Walter Dunstanville in the 13th century. This chilly, draughty old fortress was replaced in 1664 by the much more comfortable Castle Combe Manor. Although altered somewhat over the centuries, the manor still stands and has recently been converted into a luxurious hotel. And it is the manor which harbours another ghost of Castle Combe. This is an elderly woman in a long dress, who walks around the upstairs corridors at night. It is generally thought that she is a servant from many generations ago, who is pottering about to check that everything is as it should be. She is not known to have been seen since the building was converted into a hotel; so perhaps the building work has laid her finally to rest.

MALMESBURY

The charming town of Malmesbury stands on a steep, rocky hill which is hugged by the River Avon on two sides and by a tributary on a third. In his wars against the Vikings, King Alfred the Great made this a fortified town, which served as a refuge to surrounding farmers and their goods in time of trouble. It was also home to an abbey, built within the walls of the fortress town for safety from marauding Vikings.

As with all English monasteries, Malmesbury was broken up by Henry VIII and its lands and assets sold off. In part, the abbey is still roofed and is used for Christian worship to this day, but it is the ruined portion that is the centre of the hauntings. As might be expected, the ghost is that of a monk. Dressed in the usual long, grey cloak, this figure moves quietly among the broken arches and shattered stone walls of his old home. He is never seen for long. As soon as a witness gets a glimpse, he moves behind a wall or a tree and is gone.

The vast majority of monkly ghosts are anonymous. They may be any of hundreds of holy men who have occupied a particular site. But at Malmesbury there is talk that the phantom monk might be the ghost of one holy man who has earned himself both a place in history and a stained glass window in the church. This was Eilmer, who almost literally leapt into history one summer's day in 1010. Born around 980, Eilmer used his spare time between holy offices in studying God's creatures. He was particularly fascinated by birds and their power of flight. By the summer of 1010, Eilmer believed that he had fathomed the secrets of God's gift of flight. He decided to put his ideas to the test. Working alone, he constructed a contraption made of wood and fabric which he carried up to the top of the abbey tower and strapped to his arms and legs. Putting his faith in God and his own ideas, Eilmer jumped.

Whether it was by faith or skill, Eilmer did not plummet to his death. Instead he glided quite gently away from the tower, watched by his amazed brethren. After covering around 200 yards, Eilmer approached the ground and realized that, while he had thought long and hard about flight, he had paid no attention to landing. He hit the ground with a solid thump that not only smashed his wings, but also broke his leg.

As the wounded Eilmer lay in the abbey hospital, he thought about his flight at some length. He decided that what had gone wrong was that he had not put a tail on his glider. With this, he thought, he would be able to make a soft landing. Sadly, Eilmer was never able to put this very sensible idea into practice, as his abbot sternly forbade any future attempts to defy God's order and take to the air. Otherwise, Eilmer may have developed a viable glider nine centuries before the Wright Brothers achieved powered flight.

The stained glass window in Malmesbury Abbey shows Eilmer in flight; it also depicts his other claim to fame. He saw a comet as a boy in 989 and saw another in 1066, which he declared was identical to the one he had seen as a boy. We now know Eilmer was right once again. This was the comet which came to be known as Halley's Comet; its orbit brought it into view from Earth in those years.

Eilmer was clearly a remarkable man. If the ghostly monk of Malmesbury is not him, then by rights it should be.

The second of the Malmesbury ghosts lurks at the King's Arms Hotel, just down the main street from the abbey. In the early 20th century, the landlord at this ancient inn was Harry Jones, a local character. Widely known and much respected, Harry Jones died in 1920 at his beloved inn. He has returned several times since to wander the upstairs rooms. He is said to wear his distinctive hat, which never left his head, rain or shine, indoors or out. This is interesting as the real hat – as opposed to the spectral one – is preserved in the town museum. Does it disappear when the ghost appears? We do not know.

The third of Malmesbury's ghosts is rather more problematic. Many people are convinced that there is a grey lady who lurks in the street outside and in the backyard of the Old Bell Hotel. In 1889, building work uncovered the body of a young lady buried under the yard. As the pub stands right beside the burial ground, this was not inexplicable, but the body had been buried standing upright. On the other hand, there might be rather less to this ghost than meets the eye.

'Oh that old grey lady nonsense,' declared the receptionist in 2003. 'There's no such thing. We just make it up to stop the school kids from poking around the backyard on their way home

The ruined abbey of Malmesbury was the home of a remarkable monk whose daring leap earned him a place in history.

from school. We get fed up with clearing up coke cans, crisp packets, and the like. There's no ghost. It's just a story.'

One of the aforementioned school children was waiting for a bus at the front of the pub. 'Oh yeah,' he confirmed. 'That ghost woman. She's in the back of the pub. You don't want to go round there. She'll grab you if you don't watch out.'

As a story to keep children out, the grey lady seems to work. But what about the strange upright burial?

BISHOPS CANNING

The village of Bishops Canning lies nestled at the foot of the slopes that lead up to Roundway Down, but the ghosts that haunt this little place have nothing to do with the historic events which took place on the high ground. Instead they may have more to do with Bishops Canning's odd reputation for being home to the most foolish folk in Wiltshire. Why Bishops Canning should have attracted this reputation is unclear. The villagers seem just as intelligent as any other inhabitants of Wiltshire. But this has not stopped a legion of jokes and tall stories being told that begin 'There was this man from Bishops Canning. . .'

It is said that there is a mysterious entity at Bishops Canning which is able to make people do the most bizarre things. The most persistent rumour is that locals may suddenly jump out of an upstairs window, run into the road in front of a car, or do some other thing that risks personal injury. On being rescued the person mutters, 'He told me to do it,' but later can remember nothing about the events leading up to the accident.

More conventional in ghostly terms is the phantom carriage that drives through the village. The ghostly conveyance appears only at night and moves without any sound at all, seeming to glide noiselessly along the road. It is an unnerving experience to see this phantom. It is large and appears solid, but moves without sound and will vanish suddenly as if a light switch has been thrown. It is said that if the coachman is headless the sighting predicts a death in the family of the person who sees it.

The coachman has not been reported as headless recently, which is just as well for the good folk of Bishops Canning. They have enough trouble with their reputation for foolishness without also needing to worry about a death-dealing coach passing by.

OLDBURY CAMP

The mighty ramparts of Oldbury Camp rear up above the A4, south of Cherhill. Generations of travellers have recognized the fortress more by the impressive white horse carved into its flanks than by the ramparts themselves. The horse is carved on the north face of the hill, which is visible from the west, so that those coming along the A4 from Bristol have a good view of it for miles as they approach.

This particular horse is not so very old. It was cut in 1780 by the local doctor, Christopher Alsop, for no reason other than that he fancied doing so. He began his task by clambering up the impressively steep slope – it is about 1:1 – and staking out the rough outline of a horse with white flags attached to sticks. He then left a pair of workmen on the hill while he retired to a position over a half a mile away to get a good view. Using a megaphone, the good doctor, who presumably had powerful lungs, bellowed instructions to his workmen. Eventually the flags were so placed as to give a good outline of a horse. He then employed a team of workmen to cut away the turf and reveal the chalk below.

Dr Alsop added a nice touch by forming the eye of the horse out of upturned bottles buried in the ground. The sunlight, it is said, glinted and winked from the eye impressively.

In 1939, when the Second World War broke out, the Cherhill white horse was covered over so that its stark shape could not give roving German bombers their location. With the return of peace in 1945, the horse was uncovered but the glass eye had sadly gone. Today the horse is well maintained.

It is a much older ghost than the horse which lurks here and is one connected closely to the Iron Age hillfort which crowns the slopes. The

The bridleway which follows the arrow-straight course of the old Roman road over the downs climbs the slope to Oldbury Camp.

fortifications were erected in around 400 BC and kept in good repair for the next four centuries. The earthen ramparts that can be seen today were then steeper and taller, and were crowned by wooden palisades, from which defenders could hurl spears and slingstones at those unwise enough to attack.

When the Romans came to Wiltshire, Oldbury Camp was a stronghold of the local Atrebates tribe. Despite this, there is no record of a major siege or battle raging here. Perhaps, by the time the Romans reached this point, the Atrebates had already been defeated. The Romans did, however, have enough respect for both the defences of Oldbury and the fighting skills of the Atrebates to demand that the fortress be abandoned and those who lived there move to an undefended lowland site where the Roman army could keep an eye on them.

Oldbury Camp was thus abandoned, though a new Roman road was built along the southern edge of its defences. When the grip of Rome on Britain loosened and raiding began to take place, Oldbury was occupied once again.

Lowland settlements were abandoned and the fortifications of Oldbury rebuilt. The occupation was short-lived, however, for soon enough the English took over this area, and the old Roman aristocracy who had held sway were swept away.

The Roman road, however, remained in use. It is still there to this day and is in daily use as a bridleway running over the hills towards Chippenham. It cannot be confused with any of the other paths and tracks which cross these chalk hills, for it runs dead straight without regard to the steepness of the hill or the nature of the ground. And it is along this ancient road an equally ancient ghost walks. He is a Roman soldier decked out with helmet, shining breastplate, and square shield. He marches with a determined military stride as he makes his way eastward from Oldbury Camp, down the slope, and over

A modern military enthusiast of the Legio II Augusta military re-enactment group wears armour and carries equipment identical to that worn by the ghost of Oldbury Camp. The Legio II Augusta can be contacted through their website: www.legiiavg.org.uk

what is now the A361. It is here that he is seen most often, stepping out in front of cars and trucks with no regard for his own safety – and giving drivers a nasty shock as he does so. Perhaps he is still searching for his old comrades, who are long, long gone away.

BROAD HINTON

Not so very long ago there were two ghosts at Broad Hinton, but now there would appear to be only one. Even she is not so active as she once was.

The vanished ghost used to inhabit the Crown Inn, the welcoming pub with a good selection of hearty meals that stands in the centre of this village. This particular phantom was never seen, but delighted in nudging people as they drank, or tapping them from behind as they walked across the bar. The landlord in 1979 was Terry Kelley, who at first was sceptical, but later became convinced of the reality of the 'Phantom Nudger' when he himself was nudged when nobody was within sight. The current landlord knows nothing of the ghost, and it does not seem to have been reported for some 20 years.

Still about is the ghost of Lady Glanville, who has been wandering around the village for over three centuries. She is seen most often near the church of St Peter in Chains, but might be encountered almost anywhere. The church dates back to Saxon times, and two 10th-century windows show that at least some stonework of this period is left. However, the church which stands today was largely rebuilt in 1634.

Just six years after the church was built, the local landowner, Sir John Glanville, became Speaker of the House of Commons. It did him little good, however. Sir John took the side of the king when civil war broke out; so Parliament promptly threw him into prison in the Tower of London. Sir John's sons, William and Francis, picked up their swords and went to join the king's army. Francis rose rapidly to reach the rank of lieutenant colonel and was in command of his own regiment of foot by the time he was sent to Bridgwater in Somerset in 1645 to defend the city against the Parliamentarian forces based in Taunton.

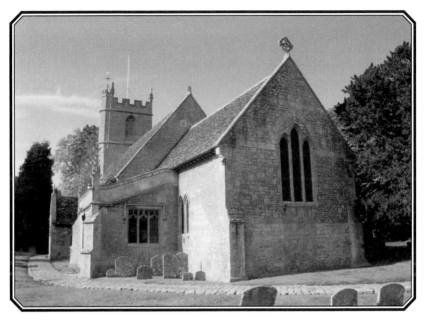

The church at Broad Hinton, near which the phantom treasure-hunter has been seen.

In May 1645, the royalists got a nasty shock when a new Parliamentarian army under none other than Oliver Cromwell arrived in front of Bridgwater. The walls were smashed down and the town fell. Young Francis was killed in the fighting. His body was brought back to Broad Hinton and buried in the church.

His distraught mother, Lady Winnifred, paid for a beautiful monument to her beloved son. He stands proudly in his armour waving the family banner above a scroll, on which is written 'A greater hero England never saw. Ah happy did she often produce his equal'. A small likeness of Lady Winnifred was included, her face stained with weeping. It is a most moving monument, which manages to be both forcefully martial and touchingly sad.

William had not been at Bridgwater, but, after the catastrophic royalist defeat at Naseby in June, he fled the country. Lady Winnifred was now alone. Her husband was in prison, her elder son in exile, and her younger son dead. It was with fear and resentment that she learned in October that Oliver Cromwell himself was coming to pay her a visit. Cromwell's visit was purely financial in motive. Parliament had declared that it should have received all taxes for the years 1644 and 1645. Those who had paid taxes to the king were deemed not to have paid at all. The Glanvilles, of course, had paid their taxes to the king. Now Cromwell was coming at the head of his men to extort the taxes again. Those who claimed to have no money to pay saw their houses stripped of silver and furniture – even the glass was taken from the windows – to pay the alleged debt.

Lady Winnifred was having none of it. She bundled the family jewels, silver, and ready cash into sacks and buried it the night before Cromwell arrived. When the Parliamentarians arrived at Broad Hinton Manor, Lady Winnifred met them at the door, carrying a burning torch. Having greeted her enemy, she turned and hurled the torch on to a pile of wood she had piled up in the hallway. The house took light in seconds and burned to the ground. Cromwell went away empty handed. Poor Lady Winnifred lost her wits and suffered a nervous and mental breakdown. She recovered somewhat when her husband was released from prison in 1648 and lived long enough to welcome her eldest son home from exile. But she never really regained her proper senses. To the great annoyance of the entire Glanville family, she could not remember where she had hidden the cash, silver, and jewellery. In her grandson's time a few coins were found near the manor. This led to some frantic digging, but nothing of any substance was ever found.

Soon after her death Lady Winnifred Glanville began to walk again. At first, she was seen near the house; later, she roamed around the fields and it was generally assumed that her distraught ghost was searching for the lost valuables of the Glanvilles. These days she appears more often near the church. Perhaps she is widening her search.

AVEBURY

The great stone circle of Avebury is one of the oldest and most impressive monuments in Wiltshire. It is also among the most haunted. The reports of ghosts around this site are many and diverse.

The ancient monument itself is the most dramatic sight in the village. It was begun in around 3000 BC, though it seems to have been altered several times in the following thousand years or so. The builders began by excavating a vast henge – a circular ditch with a bank constructed on the outside of the ring. Most henges are fairly small with shallow ditches. That at Avebury is huge. It covers 28 acres and is 500 yards across. The ditch was originally 30 feet deep and the bank over 20 feet tall. Four gaps were left in the bank and ditch facing north, south, east, and west. The chalk bedrock was hacked out with picks shaped from antlers and shovels made from ox shoulderblades. This henge alone would have taken a million and a half man-hours to construct.

Within the henge was then erected the stone circle, or rather circles. There was originally a circle of around 100 stones running around the inner side of the ditch. Within this large circle were two smaller circles, one in the northwest quadrant and another in the southeast. Not content with this mighty structure, the builders erected an avenue of standing stones that ran eastward for over a mile to a small stone circle on a hilltop. A second avenue ran to the west for another mile. Each stone was around 10 to 20 feet tall and some weighed up to 40 tons. In all, around 400 stones were erected to form the complex of Avebury.

Over the years the stones have suffered badly. In medieval times several were torn down by zealous Christians who believed they were the work of the Devil. Later, more were smashed into blocks to build houses. Even so, about a quarter remain to give an indication of the glory that was Avebury at its height.

One ghost in Avebury has echoes of the enigmatic man who appears at nearby West Kennett Long Barrow. Like the West Kennett ghost, this man is described as wearing a long, pale-coloured cloak. He is not accompanied by a dog, but otherwise seems very similar to the silent watcher seen at the ancient burial mound. Perhaps these are the phantoms of ancient holy men.

Also glimpsed flitting about the ancient stones are small figures, sometimes mistaken for children in fancy dress. Wearing loose smocks or jerkins, the little figures gambol around, as if dancing to some silent and long forgotten tune.

Standing at the heart of the stone circle is the Red Lion Inn, itself a focus of hauntings. The barmaid happily confirmed this one chill winter day towards the end of 2003. 'Oh, yes. You won't find a more active ghost than our Flori,' she declared. 'She is always about is Flori. Up to her tricks and such.' These tricks involve moving cutlery, crockery and condiments around after the staff have carefully set up the dining room for customers. She is also prone to making kitchen equipment vanish entirely, only to reappear in its proper place a day or two later. Flori's favourite trick, however, is to set the ceiling lights swinging violently from side to side, casting strange shadows as the lights twirl above the bar.

The ancient standing stones of Avebury attract more than one phantom visitor.

Flori herself is seen less often than her little tricks are performed. When she does show herself, she is a young woman with long, dark hair, who appears dressed in a long, flowing skirt and tight bodice with wrist length, snug sleeves. Apart from a wide white collar, all her clothes are uniformly dark. It is believed that Flori was the wife of the inn owner back in the 1640s. He went off to fight in the civil war and, on his return, found Flori in the arms of another man. In

The Red Lion at Avebury is haunted by one of Wiltshire's most active ghosts.

a fit of jealousy he killed them both, then answered for his crimes on the scaffold. Now Flori comes back to her old home alone. She visits quite often and, like many ghosts, appears to be solid and real to those who see her. In the 1970s one diner even tried to order his dessert from her. She takes no notice of living humans, however, always walking briskly from one room to another and vanishing from sight.

A second ghost haunts the Red Lion, but this ghost may have rather more to do with nearby Avebury Manor. A carriage and pair of horses appears on the drive of the manor, leaves through the wrought iron gates, and trots briskly through the village until it reaches the Red Lion, where it suddenly vanishes from sight. The manor has another ghost, which is all its own. A man in a wide-brimmed hat is sometimes seen in the garden of the manor. Those who have glimpsed him think he might be a cavalier, but sightings are too fleeting to be sure.

WEST KENNETT LONG BARROW

Standing alone on a windswept hill just south of the A4 Great West Road is the ancient burial mound now known as West Kennett Long Barrow. It is visited by many tourists and passers-by, but there is one visitor far older than any other. He has been coming here for the past 5,000 years.

The long barrow is a mound of grass-covered earth, which is over 100 yards long and stands some 10 feet tall. When it was first built, around 3250 BC, it would have been rather taller, and its walls of white chalk would have stood out stark and bold against the green turf of the hills. The eastern end of the barrow, facing sunrise, is marked by several huge sarsen boulders set on end.

The impressive facade of West Kennett Long Barrow, haunted by a ghost which appears only at dawn.

These close the entrance to the burial chamber within, which takes the form of a long passage with five side chambers. The burial ground was in use for generations, serving as a communal tomb for the local folk who built and maintained it.

The only people likely to see the ghost of West Kennett are farmers or others who get up rather earlier than is the norm these days. He appears outside the eastern end of the barrow at dawn. Tall and dressed in a white cloak, this old man stands to face the sunrise. At his side is a large, powerful dog with a white shaggy coat and reddish ears. Silently, this strange pair watch the sun come up over the Marlborough Downs; then they turn and enter the tomb. They are, presumably, the phantoms of a priest from ancient times and his dog. Or perhaps the tall man is the ghost of one of those buried within. Whoever he is, this man and his dog must qualify as among the oldest ghosts in Britain.

WROUGHTON

The hillside village of Wroughton has the unique distinction in Wiltshire of being the location of a haunted tree. The tree in question stands in the churchyard at the top of the hill and is an ancient yew. It is a mighty tree with branches that spread out over 60 feet and cover an area of over 2,500 square feet.

Opinions are divided as to exactly what haunts this tree. One theory holds that it is the ghost of a man who committed suicide by hanging himself from its branches, the sin of suicide being made all the worse for being carried out on holy ground. Another idea is that the phantom is a woman buried in the churchyard, who died with a guilty secret.

All are agreed, however, that the way to raise the ghost is to run three times round the yew tree's trunk without drawing breath. How one should go about persuading the ghost to go away again, once having raised it, seems to be something not considered. It is probably best to leave this ghost where it is.

The giant yew tree of Wroughton, around which mystery swirls.

SWINDON

In its heyday, Lydiard House was one of the most charming stately homes in Wiltshire. It is relatively small and very homely, despite its grand Palladian style. The surrounding grounds were landscaped in the 18th century to include a small lake, an arboretum, and extensive sweeping lawns. The estate is now in the hands of Swindon Council, which cares for it very well. The park is open every day, together with its café and visitors' centre, and the house and adjacent chapel are open most days.

The house lies at the centre of the hauntings. It was built for Sir John St John, whose family had then owned the estate for over two centuries. The baronet's life was to be marked by tragedy. He was a staunch royalist who lost three sons to the cause during the Civil War, and then, when the war was over,

The elegant facade of Lydiard House, Swindon, where a sad ghost of a man who led a melancholy life returns to haunt his old home.

he was reduced to penury by the vengeful Parliament. It took decades for the family to rebuild its fortunes – the title and estates passing to a junior branch.

To commemorate his eldest boy, Sir John had erected in the chapel at Lydiard a monument that has since become famous as the Golden Cavalier. This takes the form of a life-size effigy of Edward St John emerging from his campaign tent dressed in cavalry armour and grasping a shield bearing the family coat of arms. The entire figure is gilded, hence the monument's name.

With such a life of woe, it is perhaps not surprising that Sir John haunts this place. The kindly old gentleman is seen pottering around the grounds close to the house at all times of day and night. A former warden of the house, Joyce Ingram, says 'We can always tell when he is about. The temperature drops dramatically and there is this distinctive, sweet smell.' It is to be hoped that Sir John is happier as a ghost than he was in life.

Elsewhere in Swindon is the Clifton Hotel. During the 1980s this was the scene of some fairly dramatic poltergeist activity, but it seems to be quiet enough these days.

HIGHWORTH

L ike so many places in Wiltshire, Highworth received its fair share of damage during the Civil War. As a hilltop town, Highworth was fortified by the local royalists, but only in desultory fashion. When Oliver Cromwell arrived in 1645, he needed only to fire his cannon a few times for the defenders to realize they were seriously outgunned and then surrender.

One of Cromwell's cannon scored a hit on St Michael's church, causing an ugly scar in the stonework that remains to this day. The culprit cannonball is preserved inside the church.

Whether the ghost that lurks in the churchyard has anything to do with the fighting that left its mark here is unknown. Those who see it do not have time to notice much about this rather vague figure, other than its eyes. They are dark, sinister, and somehow mesmerizing. Then the spectre is gone before there is time to note its costume or appearance.

The ghost at the King and Queen Inn in the High Street is rather better known. The pub was built in the 14th century as a guesthouse for visitors to the monastery that then stood in the town. After the Reformation it became a pub, but one of its monastic residents has never left. Legend has it that the monk who kept the guesthouse used his lodgings outside the monastery walls to keep trysts with a lover. When the abbot found out that the monk had broken his vows of celibacy, the unfortunate sinner was promptly hanged.

Be that as it may, the ghost seen at the pub is most definitely that of a man dressed in monkish robes of a pale cream colour. He has been seen in several places and is heard moving around in the attic when no one is there. A sighting in 2002 had him walking through the bar from front to back in the middle of the afternoon. In the 1960s the then landlord saw what he thought was an intruder in the yard and set his dog on the figure. The dog took a step or two forward, halted, and then bolted. The strange figure meanwhile glided silently across the yard and suddenly faded from view. This is not the only dog to dislike the ghost. More than one dog brought into the pub to accompany the owner for a drink has suddenly become uneasy, whimpering in fright or barking ferociously at what seems to be a blank wall. Dogs, it seems, are more attuned to seeing ghosts than are humans.

CHISELDON

Nobody has seen the bizarre phantom of Chiseldon for some years. This might be as well, for it was a strange and disturbing apparition.

The village stands on a hill overlooking a steep, narrow valley, overgrown with trees, brambles, and general undergrowth. A path runs from the church down into the ravine and west to the village of Hodson. It was along this path that the ghost used to appear. The ghost had no defined shape, being likened to a sack full of water by one observer. It seemed to bob along, a couple of feet above the ground, and then vanish.

The steps that lead down to the haunted path of Chiseldon.

OGBOURNE ST ANDREW

The church of Ogbourne St Andrew, a place noted for its brooding atmosphere.

There is something very strange at Ogbourne St Andrew, but nobody is entirely certain what it is. Whatever it is, it lurks near the church of St Andrew. This stands on an unusual site for a Christian church, for it lies close beside a large and ancient round barrow. Most round barrows are quite small, but this one has an impressively large bulk, which is made all the larger by the trees and dense undergrowth with which it is covered. The place has a brooding quality and the atmosphere of there being a definite 'something' about it. Tales are varied about what it is that is seen here, but all agree that the spectre is unpleasant.

Not far away from the barrow is a little ravine by the name of Poughcombe, where the Devil is said to sleep when he is visiting Wiltshire. It may be that the stories that cluster about Ogbourne St Andrew are faint traces of the old pagan religion which held sway here centuries ago. The great barrow is undoubtedly a pagan monument, and the early church would have labelled a pagan god as a devil so the devil that sleeps at Poughcombe might be some old, old deity, resentful at being ignored.

UPAVON

The phantom creature of Upavon is a strange beast, which might, just possibly, be a real animal rather than a spectre. It first began to be seen in 1992, and, off and on, it has been reported ever since.

The beast is usually caught sight of in the fields around the village, rather than in the built up area itself. Once, however, it ventured into the vicarage garden. The descriptions of the animal are fairly consistent and describe a grey

The quiet meadows around Upavon where a mysterious beast has been seen.

creature, about the size of a wolfhound, but with a distinctly cat-like shape and movements. Some have suggested that it is a puma or similar predator which has escaped from a zoo or circus. No such cat has been reported missing, nor is it clear why an escaped big cat would spend some years lurking close to just one village rather than wandering far and wide in search of food.

Despite some clear and credible sightings of this odd animal, there is little hard proof of either its physical existence or spectral status, and it must be marked down as being something of an unknown.

PEWSEY

Pewsey has two ghosts: one a remarkably annoying one, and the other quite gentle. They have their homes at opposite ends of this little town, which is an odd mix of ancient thatched cottages and grand Georgian town houses. The more friendly of the two ghosts frequents a shop on the southern side of

Pewsey High Street is haunted by a genteel Victorian lady.

High Street. She is a woman in a dress which seems to date her to the early Victorian period. Nobody is quite sure who she is, but, as is so often the case, she appears to be quite solid and real when she is first seen. This person seems to have a particular affinity with the staircase, for she is seen most often either walking down it or loitering at its foot.

More energetic was the poltergeist which plagued the Crown Inn during the 1980s. This entity was less violent than some poltergeists, there being no reports of fires or injuries, but it was very active. It threw objects around with enthusiasm and took particular delight in snatching bedclothes off sleeping people. For some reason the poltergeist took a dislike to an antique pistol that was hung in the bar. The pistol was never allowed to stay still from one day to the next. It might be thrown to the floor, hidden upstairs, or simply spun round. As is the way with poltergeists, the phenomenon gradually tailed off after a few months. The Crown is now as quiet as it is welcoming.

NORTH TIDWORTH

The small town of Tidworth is famous in the records of the paranormal for being the scene of a notorious, violent, and early haunting. Although the events took place in 1661, they were investigated by interested gentlemen and careful records were kept of what went on. Quite clearly this was an early example of a poltergeist at large in Wiltshire, though at the time nobody knew what it was. Instead they called it the Demon Drummer of Tidworth, and its fame spread throughout the kingdom.

The trouble centred on the home of John Mompesson, the local magistrate. While Mompesson was in London on business, his wife and servants heard an odd knocking noise coming from outside the house after dark, as if someone was banging two pieces of wood together. On the fourth night, Mompesson was at home. When the noises began he dashed outside armed with his pistols, but the noises ended and nobody was to be seen. Two nights later the source of the noises changed to the roof, as if an invisible person was banging on the tiles. Eight nights later the sound entered the house.

The village signpost at Tidworth shows the demon drummer who made this place famous three centuries ago.

This time the strange noises came from a large drum that was being stored in a downstairs lumber room. It was this that gave the phantom his name. For hour upon hour, the drum played itself. Rolls, tattoos, and marches sounded out from the drum as if an invisible demon was beating it with gusto.

The drum had belonged to a vagrant named William Drury, who had been arrested some weeks earlier on charges of causing a nuisance by harassing people with his drum while begging. Drury had claimed that he was an invalided soldier and that beating the drum was his old regimental duty. Mompesson had sent a letter to the regiment's colonel to ask for confirmation of Drury's story and had impounded the drum until he got an answer. Drury, meanwhile, had fled.

It was now assumed that Drury had used witchcraft to put a curse on the

Mompesson household for having taken his drum. Messengers were sent out far and wide asking the authorities to arrest Drury and return him to Tidworth. Mompesson took advantage of a break in the demon drumming to have the drum taken outside and burnt.

He gained no relief. The banging and thumping returned, now being carried out on random pieces of furniture and floorboards. The noises came only at night. Concerned for the safety of his children, Mompesson moved them to the attic, but the noises followed them. It was now becoming clear that the noises were always centred around the children, in particular, on the eldest teenage daughter. Indeed, the sounds came only when she was asleep.

It was now more than two months since the disturbances had begun. Suddenly they took on a new and more frightening manifestation. Invisible hands began to throw objects around the house. Mrs Mompesson had her hair pulled, an attack that was soon repeated on the children.

Six months into the bizarre and worrying events, help appeared in the form of a court official sent down from London by King Charles II himself. Equipped with a bag of money and full royal powers, this official had been instructed by Charles to investigate the strange stories that had reached London, and, just as important, to sort the matter out. Just a few days after this worthy arrived, a dark figure with glowing red eyes was seen hovering above the floorboards in Tidworth House. Declaring it to be a devil, Mr Mompesson let fly with a musket. The devil vanished, and for several days peace reigned. The official hurried back to tell the king what had occurred and make his report, from which we know so much about this haunting. But the demon drummer soon returned, more active and apparently angrier than ever.

Three months later the beggar Drury was finally tracked down. He had been arrested in Yorkshire for stealing a pig. Although he gave a false name, he was recognized and sent back to Tidworth under armed guard. The vagrant was put on trial for witchcraft and the court heard all the evidence of the hauntings and the actions of the demon drummer. In an outbreak of common sense – rather unusual in the 17th century when it came to witchcraft trials – Drury was found not guilty. He had already been found guilty of pig theft and sentenced to two years of hard labour in His Majesty's colonies in the West

Indies. Within a few days of Drury's being put on board ship in chains, the demon drummer left Tidworth, never to return.

For the Mompesson family and those who tried to help them, the demon drummer was a terrifying and bizarre experience. They blamed the vagrant Drury because the trouble centred on his drum and because the noises so often resembled drumming. It now seems unlikely that Drury had anything to do with it.

Poltergeists indulge in exactly the sorts of activity described in this case. Moreover, they almost invariably occur when a teenager, usually a girl, is undergoing emotional turmoil of some kind. The Mompessons had just had a new baby, and the event may have upset the eldest daughter in some way. Similarly, poltergeists are known to start gradually, build up to a peak of activity, and then fade away after a few months, just as the demon drummer did.

Of course, nobody has yet managed to produce a credible explanation of exactly what causes a poltergeist event to occur. Perhaps the troubled teenager somehow causes the events by some form of unconscious mind power, or he or she may attract a mischievous spirit from some other world. Sceptics argue that the teenager is tricking everyone and causing the events to gain attention and sympathy. Put simply poltergeists are unexplained, but although they are noisy, frightening, and occasionally able to break objects, they rarely, if ever, cause any actual harm to anyone. Like the Demon Drummer of Tidworth they come, create mayhem, and then go away again.

In 1836 a second and much less troublesome ghost came to the area. A chance discovery led to the unearthing of a Roman villa a little to the north of Tidworth. The excavation was good by the standards of the day and thorough. A beautiful mosaic was revealed and was lifted stone by stone to be transported to the British Museum where it still lies. The digging seems to have disturbed the spirits of those associated with the site. For many years afterwards, a Roman soldier was seen to march near the remains of the villa. He has not been sighted much in recent years, but does still put in the odd appearance.

CHUTE

hute Causeway stands on the border between Wiltshire and Hampshire. It is haunted by a guilty spirit who has much to atone for, but he is doing his best, and it must be hoped that one day he will achieve forgiveness for his sins.

The story belongs to the dread year 1665, when the plague stalked England. The plague was, and is, a dreadful disease, but in 1665 it seemed far worse, as people had no idea how it spread or how to combat it once it was caught. The death toll was high: around half of those who caught it would die, and an infected community would typically lose between 10% and 30% of its population.

The old road of Chute Causeway, where a vicar returns to atone for his mortal sins committed in the 17th century.

The symptoms were the stuff of nightmare. The first sign of infection was normally a fever, followed by a dry tongue coated in a soft white fur. Vomiting came next, followed by an intense thirst. By this time – around six hours after the fever began – the victim started to feel painful lumps forming in the armpits and groin areas. These grew rapidly and within 12 hours were the size of golfballs, while the mouth was filled with a thick brown mucus. Within another 12 hours the swellings turned black and were astonishingly painful. This was the moment of decision. Those destined to die developed a rapidly soaring fever and slipped into a trance-like coma, which ended in death a few hours later. Those who lived hovered in agony for days until the swellings and fever subsided. Some people found their health was permanently broken by an attack of plague, so that they fell an easy victim to any later disease or infection. A few victims developed a form of the plague which attacked the lungs instead of the bloodstream. These people died quickly after a few blood-spattered coughs showed they were ill. Some went to bed healthy and died before midnight.

It is now known the cause of plague is a bacterium carried by rat fleas. A general improvement in hygiene and the extermination of rats from human habitations has eradicated the plague. But in the 17th century it was a dreadful and inexplicable visitation.

When the plague came to Vernham Dean, the villagers were understandably terrified, as was everyone who lived in the area. At gunpoint, each villager who showed symptoms was herded up to the hilltop above Chute Causeway and told to stay there until they died or the plague left them. Only the vicar was allowed to come down from the hill top every third day to bring out money and to carry back food and supplies. Three times the vicar performed this duty as the plague took its firm and hideous grip on his flock. But, on his fourth trip, the poor man found he could muster the moral strength to return to the disease-ridden hell on the hilltop no longer. He fled. Starvation was added to the misery of the plague camp as the supplies dried up. There were no survivors.

It is the guilt-wracked ghost of the errant vicar who plods slowly from Vernham Dean, along Chute Causeway, and up to the fatal summit. He is bowed down with a heavy sack of supplies for those he failed in life. But no sack could be as heavy as the weight of his remorse. It is not wise to interrupt this ghost, for he must do his penance in full before, it is to be hoped, he finally finds peace and rest.

LITTLECOTE

Perhaps the most famous ghost story in Wiltshire revolves around Littlecote House, which stands only a few feet from the site of a Roman villa. The mansion itself is a fine example of early Tudor architecture, which has not been altered much in the intervening centuries. It was built in the 1510s for the local Darrell family, but was destined not to stay with that family for long. The reason has much to do with the hauntings.

One winter's night in 1575 the local midwife and nurse, Mrs Barnes, was awoken at her home in Great Shefford in Berkshire by a man whose face was muffled by a scarf. Behind him was a coach and four, on which a coat of arms had been hurriedly painted out. The man asked her to come with him to attend a sick lady. He offered her a large purse of gold on condition that she ask no questions and never tell anyone of the patient or the journey. Not being overendowed with money, Mrs Barnes agreed. She was promptly blindfolded and bundled into the coach.

After some hours of travelling the coach stopped and she was led, still blindfolded, across a gravel drive and up some steps into a warm house. After negotiating a flight of stairs, Mrs Barnes was allowed to remove the blindfold. She found herself in a sumptuous bedroom warmed by a blazing log fire. In the bed was a woman who was obviously well into labour and about to give birth. A pair of elderly women hovered nearby, but were clearly out of their depth. In the corner stood a tall dark man.

Mrs Barnes guessed she had stumbled on some family scandal. Perhaps the pregnant lady was the daughter of the house who had become pregnant by a servant; perhaps she was the squire's mistress. Whatever the reason, thought Mrs Barnes, the ways of the gentry were not her business. She would deliver the baby, take her money, and go home.

Things did not work out that way. As soon as the baby was born, the dark man snatched it from Mrs Barnes's hands, and, despite the screams of the mother, threw it into the fire, holding it down with his boot until it died. While this horrific scene was played out, Mrs Barnes hurriedly cut a corner of fabric from the bed hangings. Again blindfolded, Mrs Barnes was led out to the coach, but this time she counted the number of stairs on the staircase.

The next day Mrs Barnes went straight to her local magistrate, Sir John Popham. The number of stairs narrowed down the number of large houses nearby that could have been the scene of the brutal infanticide. And the piece of fabric quickly confirmed that Littlecote was the house in question. Mrs Barnes at once identified the squire, Sir William Darrell, as the killer. Darrell was a notorious rake, drinker, and debauchee. Popham charged him with the killing, but Darrell was destined never to come to trial.

Out riding one day soon after, Darrell was thrown from his horse and broke his neck. The man with him swore that he heard a baby crying at the moment Wild Will fell. The spot is still known as Darrell's stile and it is haunted to this day by the tall dark form of Wild Will Darrell, mounted on his powerful black stallion and galloping at high speed down the lane. The spot is actually over the border in Berkshire; so the apparition may not qualify as a Wiltshire ghost geographically.

Littlecote House is, however, definitely in Wiltshire and it is haunted by both Wild Will and by the mother and baby. As the matter never came to trial, it was not publicly announced who the lady in question actually was. One theory holds that it was Darrell's own sister, but another theory says she was the wife of a neighbouring landowner named Sir Henry Knyvett, who had fallen for the evil charms of Darrell. Whoever she was, her ghost has been seen wandering distraught through the corridors of Littlecote, a tiny baby in her arms.

The gardens are haunted by another woman. She is dressed in the fashion of about a century after the time of Wild Will; so this restless spirit is not connected to the frightful events of that winter evening. Who she might be is unknown, but she seems peaceful enough as she wanders around among the flowers.